PROPOSED FEDERAL WATER GRABS AND THEIR POTENTIAL IMPACTS ON STATES, WATER AND POWER USERS, AND LANDOWNERS

OVERSIGHT HEARING

BEFORE THE

SUBCOMMITTEE ON WATER, POWER AND OCEANS

OF THE

COMMITTEE ON NATURAL RESOURCES
U.S. HOUSE OF REPRESENTATIVES

ONE HUNDRED FOURTEENTH CONGRESS

FIRST SESSION

Tuesday, April 14, 2015

Serial No. 114–1

Printed for the use of the Committee on Natural Resources

Available via the World Wide Web: http://www.fdsys.gov
or
Committee address: http://naturalresources.house.gov

U.S. GOVERNMENT PUBLISHING OFFICE

94–271 PDF   WASHINGTON : 2015

For sale by the Superintendent of Documents, U.S. Government Publishing Office
Internet: bookstore.gpo.gov   Phone: toll free (866) 512–1800; DC area (202) 512–1800
Fax: (202) 512–2104   Mail: Stop IDCC, Washington, DC 20402–0001

COMMITTEE ON NATURAL RESOURCES

ROB BISHOP, UT, *Chairman*
RAÚL M. GRIJALVA, AZ, *Ranking Democratic Member*

Don Young, AK
Louie Gohmert, TX
Doug Lamborn, CO
Robert J. Wittman, VA
John Fleming, LA
Tom McClintock, CA
Glenn Thompson, PA
Cynthia M. Lummis, WY
Dan Benishek, MI
Jeff Duncan, SC
Paul A. Gosar, AZ
Raúl R. Labrador, ID
Doug LaMalfa, CA
Bradley Byrne, AL
Jeff Denham, CA
Paul Cook, CA
Bruce Westerman, AR
Garret Graves, LA
Dan Newhouse, WA
Ryan K. Zinke, MT
Jody B. Hice, GA
Aumua Amata Coleman Radewagen, AS
Thomas MacArthur, NJ
Alexander X. Mooney, WV
Cresent Hardy, NV

Grace F. Napolitano, CA
Madeleine Z. Bordallo, GU
Jim Costa, CA
Gregorio Kilili Camacho Sablan, CNMI
Niki Tsongas, MA
Pedro R. Pierluisi, PR
Jared Huffman, CA
Raul Ruiz, CA
Alan S. Lowenthal, CA
Matt Cartwright, PA
Donald S. Beyer, Jr., VA
Norma J. Torres, CA
Debbie Dingell, MI
Mark Takai, HI
Ruben Gallego, AZ
Lois Capps, CA
Jared Polis, CO

Jason Knox, *Chief of Staff*
Lisa Pittman, *Chief Counsel*
David Watkins, *Democratic Staff Director*
Sarah Parker, *Democratic Deputy Chief Counsel*

————

SUBCOMMITTEE ON WATER, POWER AND OCEANS

JOHN FLEMING, LA, *Chairman*
JARED HUFFMAN, CA, *Ranking Democratic Member*

Don Young, AK
Robert J. Wittman, VA
Tom McClintock, CA
Cynthia M. Lummis, WY
Jeff Duncan, SC
Paul A. Gosar, AZ
Doug LaMalfa, CA
Bradley Byrne, AL
Jeff Denham, CA
Dan Newhouse, WA
Thomas MacArthur, NJ
Rob Bishop, UT, *ex officio*

Grace F. Napolitano, CA
Jim Costa, CA
Ruben Gallego, AZ
Madeleine Z. Bordallo, GU
Gregorio Kilili Camacho Sablan, CNMI
Raul Ruiz, CA
Alan S. Lowenthal, CA
Norma J. Torres, CA
Debbie Dingell, MI
Raúl M. Grijalva, AZ, *ex officio*

————

CONTENTS

OVERSIGHT HEARING ON PROPOSED FEDERAL WATER GRABS AND THEIR POTENTIAL IMPACTS ON STATES, WATER AND POWER USERS, AND LANDOWNERS

Tuesday, April 14, 2015
U.S. House of Representatives
Subcommittee on Water, Power and Oceans
Committee on Natural Resources
Washington, DC

The subcommittee met, pursuant to notice, at 1:53 p.m., in room 1324, Longworth House Office Building, Hon. John Fleming [Chairman of the Subcommittee] presiding.

Present: Representatives Fleming, McClintock, Lummis, Gosar, LaMalfa, Newhouse, MacArthur; Huffman, Napolitano, and Costa.

Also present: Representatives Tipton, Westerman, Graves, and Zinke.

Dr. FLEMING. The Subcommittee on Water, Power, and Oceans will come to order. The Water, Power, and Oceans Subcommittee meets today to hear testimony on a hearing entitled, ''Proposed Federal Water Grabs and Their Potential Impacts on States, Water and Power Users, and Landowners.''

Before we begin, I ask unanimous consent to allow our colleagues, Congressmen Westerman, Graves, Zinke, and Tipton to participate in our hearing today.

[No response.]

Dr. FLEMING. Hearing no objection, so ordered.

We will begin with 5-minute opening statements by myself and the Ranking Member, Congressman Huffman of California. I now recognize myself for opening statement.

STATEMENT OF THE HON. JOHN FLEMING, A REPRESENTATIVE IN CONGRESS FROM THE STATE OF LOUISIANA

Dr. FLEMING. Today the Subcommittee on Water, Power, and Oceans meets to review Federal proposals that could increase water and power rates, and help perpetuate drought.

Adequate and reliable water supplies are necessary for our continued success as a Nation. Historically, most of our water resources have been managed at the state and local levels, and rightly so. Even Federal dams and reservoirs deliver water based on the premise of state-granted water rights. Many have experienced firsthand the frustration of the Federal Endangered Species Act and other Federal laws overriding state water rights. Indeed, this administration has pushed the envelope with proposals aimed at superseding historical state and local water actions.

It has a history of rolling out ill-explained and ill-informed Washington, DC-Knows-Best proposals in recent years, only to stand down later, after hearing backlash from the public. The so-

(1)

called Blueways Program was the first, followed by the ski areas water clause, then followed by the Forest Service's Groundwater Directive, which could have impacted 155 national forests, including the Kisatchie in Louisiana.

The people who depend on multiple uses of our waters and public lands have felt they have played the Whack-a-Mole game with these administration proposals. There seems to be no end in sight.

These proposals, and the Waters of the U.S. regulations sitting at the White House now, have been drafted on the guise of 'clarifying' the authority of Federal agencies. Only in Washington, DC would 'clarification' mean Federal expansion. The end result could be Federal jurisdiction over ditches and other water bodies currently regulated at the state and local levels, and regulatory chaos.

These proposals would be a litigant's dream and a private property owner's nightmare, and potentially, higher water and power rates, which we will hear about today.

Throughout today we will hear about the Administration's inability to communicate with those most affected by these proposals. The EPA and the Forest Service have reacted with what some have termed ''apology tours.'' It begs the question of why they failed to engage our Nation's governors, water users, and others in the first place, to help avoid this mess.

The witnesses before us today represent some of the stakeholders who were forgotten in the Federal agency process. I would especially like to welcome the hard-working folks from the National Water Resources Association, many of which are in the audience today. They see firsthand how these proposals will impact the water customers they serve.

It is telling, from what the President called ''the most transparent administration in history,'' that the Federal agency NWRA's members primarily work with, the Bureau of Reclamation, refused to show up and answer questions about the potential impacts of these proposals.

I would also like to welcome Mr. Mike Heinen—I hope I am saying that right—the General Manager of the Jeff Davis Electric Cooperative in Jennings, Louisiana, for being here today. Did I say that right? Heinen, I am sorry. It was a 50/50 chance, and, of course, I got it wrong. I commend Mike for his efforts to keep the lights on for Louisianans, and for telling his story on how these proposals will make it harder for him to do so.

It is simply time for these Federal agencies to start over and do it right. Communication with the American people is the first step.

[The prepared statement of Dr. Fleming follows:]

PREPARED STATEMENT OF THE HON. JOHN FLEMING, CHAIRMAN, SUBCOMMITTEE ON WATER, POWER AND OCEANS

Today, the Subcommittee on Water, Power and Oceans meets to review Federal proposals that could increase water and power rates and help perpetuate drought.

Adequate and reliable water supplies are necessary for our continued success as a Nation.

Historically, most of our water resources have been managed at the state and local levels—and rightly so. Even Federal dams and reservoirs deliver water based on the premise of state-granted water rights.

While the Federal Endangered Species Act and some Federal laws continue to override some of those state water rights, this administration has pushed the envelope with proposals aimed at super-ceding historical state and local water actions.

The Administration has a history of rolling out ill-explained and ill-informed Washington, DC-knows-best proposals in recent years only to stand down later after hearing backlash from the public. The so-called Blueways program was the first, followed by the ski areas water clause, then followed by the Forest Service's Groundwater Directive which could have impacted 155 national forests, including the Kisatchie in Louisiana.

The people who depend on multiple uses of our waters and public lands have felt they've played the Whack-a-Mole game with these administration proposals. There seems to be no end in sight.

These proposals—and the Waters-of-the-U.S. regulation sitting at the White House now—have been drafted under the guise of quote ''clarifying'' unquote the authority of Federal agencies. Only in Washington, DC would 'clarification' mean Federal expansion. The end result could be Federal jurisdiction over ditches and other water bodies currently regulated at the state and local levels and regulatory chaos.

These proposals would be a litigant's dream and a private property owner's nightmare . . . and potentially higher water and power rates which we will hear about today.

Throughout today, we will hear about the Administration's inability to communicate with those most affected by these proposals. The EPA and the Forest Service have reacted with what some have termed apology tours. It begs the question of why they failed to engage our Nation's Governors, water users and others in the first place to help avoid this mess.

The witnesses before us today represent some of the stakeholders who were forgotten in the Federal agency process. I would especially like to welcome the hardworking folks from the National Water Resources Association, many of which are in the audience today. They see firsthand how these proposals will impact the water customers they serve.

It's telling from what the President called ''the most transparent administration in history'' that the Federal agency NWRA's members primarily work with—the Bureau of Reclamation—refused to show up and answer questions about the potential impacts of these proposals.

I would also like to welcome Mr. Mike Heinen, the General Manager of the Jeff Davis Electric Cooperative in Jennings, Louisiana for being here today. I commend Mike for his efforts to keep the lights on for Louisianans and for telling his story on how these proposals will make it harder for him to do so.

It's simply time for these Federal agencies to start over and do it right. Communication with the American people is the first step.

————

Dr. FLEMING. OK. We are still waiting on the Ranking Member. So the Chair now recognizes the Vice Chair, the gentleman from Arizona, for his opening statement.

STATEMENT OF THE HON. PAUL A. GOSAR, A REPRESENTATIVE IN CONGRESS FROM THE STATE OF ARIZONA

Dr. GOSAR. Thank you very much, Mr. Chairman. Our subcommittee meets today to conduct oversight on expansive Federal regulations that ignore the primary role of the states in regulating groundwater and issuing water rights. For those of us in the West, state water laws and the rights that they protect are paramount to our economy, our environment, and our way of life.

Westerners suffer from drought on a constant basis, which is why we have invested in water storage and delivery projects that supply water and hydropower in dry times. The proposals before us today will erode those benefits.

Nearly a year ago, we held a hearing on this very same topic. While the Forest Service has temporarily withdrawn its unnecessary groundwater directive, states, localities, and private entities still face regulatory uncertainty under the shadow of the Federal Government. Instead of creating clarity, this administration has created chaos.

This is not new, however. Three years ago, the people of the White River Watershed in Arkansas and Missouri learned that 250-feet Federal buffer zones were part of a federally designated blueway regulatory blueprint. At the same time, the Forest Service tried to extort privately held water rights by holding public use permits for ski resorts captive.

Last year, the Forest Service proposed a sweeping groundwater directive under the guise of eliminating future litigation. That directive only caused further confusion and potential litigation. We will hear today from the bipartisan Western Governors' Association that the directives asserted new Federal ownership of groundwater, and how there was little to no communication with any of those impacted by the document.

You will also hear how the proposed Waters of the U.S. proposal could impact state-based groundwater regulations, and make it even harder for Westerners suffering from serious drought to finish groundwater recharge and conservation projects aimed at eliminating drought.

Based on these repeated actions, clearly, this administration is out of touch with those who work, care for, and preserve our waters and lands. The Obama administration has made it clear that it has no intention of following the law or respecting the legislative process when developing Federal rules and regulations. This President has repeatedly chosen to ignore the will of the people, American people, and govern by executive fiat to implement his far-left ideology. And that is why legislation is necessary for long-term certainty.

The House passed Congressman Scott Tipton's bill last year to limit these excessive Federal attempts that undermine long-held state water laws, and I look forward to working with him and others this year to pass similar legislation.

I also introduced Waters of the United States Regulatory Overreach Protection Act earlier this year. This bipartisan bill requires the relevant Federal agencies to go back to the drawing board and consult with states and other local officials to formulate a proposal. Everyone wants clean water. But crafting regulations without first speaking with stakeholders is a foolish approach in good governance.

We are privileged today to hear from several witnesses impacted firsthand by these proposals. I also want to welcome those from the National Water Resources Association, who have traveled to Washington, DC to protect and grow their local regional economies. Thank you for your hard work.

I look forward to today's testimony and moving forward on efforts to resolve these issues. I yield back the balance of my time, Mr. Chairman.

Dr. FLEMING. The gentleman yields back.

The Chair now recognizes Ranking Member, Mr. Huffman.

STATEMENT OF THE HON. JARED HUFFMAN, A REPRESENTATIVE IN CONGRESS FROM THE STATE OF CALIFORNIA

Mr. HUFFMAN. Thank you, Mr. Chairman. I apologize that I was a little slow getting back. I have a boot on my left foot, and I am not quite as mobile as I would like to be right now.

I want to welcome our witnesses today to discuss the proposed definition of "Waters of the United States" under the Clean Water Act, and also the Forest Service's previously proposed groundwater directive, which—we know, but bears emphasis—was put on hold in February.

I think, Mr. Chair and Mr. Vice Chair, we have a very constructive start on the committee and subcommittee this year. We had a reasonable budget hearing. We discussed real issues. It was respectful, it was constructive, and I am pleased and encouraged by the conversations that I have had with each of you about opportunities to work together this year on items of mutual interest. And that is why I am disappointed that today's hearing is a step backward to the partisan warfare of the last Congress, complete with a loaded, inflammatory title to this particular hearing.

A similar hearing in the last Congress was called, "Federal Schemes to Soak up Water Authority." This time it is about so-called water grabs. I am sorry to say this approach is premised on a straw man argument that the Obama administration is somehow bent on a radical, power-hungry quest to illegally assert authority over virtually every drop of water in the country. That is nonsense.

The simple reality is that the draft administration proposal we are discussing today on the jurisdiction of the Clean Water Act is very narrowly tailored. Under President Ronald Reagan, hardly a radical, big-government expansionist, hardly an environmentalist, the Clean Water Act covered any body of water that could serve as habitat for migratory birds, a much more far-reaching standard than the one the Obama administration is currently considering.

The GAO determined in 2004 that the Reagan clean water rule would have allowed the Army Corps to regulate almost any body of water or wetland. Let's remember that when we hear the characterizations that the Obama administration's draft proposal is some unprecedented overreach of executive power. It raises the question whether this concern about the proposed rule, which is far narrower than the Ronald Reagan rule, is about the substance, or is it more about who happens to be in the White House right now.

Mr. Chairman, many of the concerns that are expressed in the testimony from today's witnesses have been expressed in other committees. In addition to serving on this committee, I serve on the Transportation and Infrastructure Committee, which actually has jurisdiction over the Clean Water Act—this committee does not—raising another question about whether this is about the substance of the clean water rule, or just another chance to attack the Obama administration.

Question after question about this rule has been posed on whether it would expand Federal authority, require new permitting. The Administration has been asked specifically multiple times about ditches on mine sites, prior converted crop lands, wastewater treatment, other ditches, uplands, artificial lakes, a channel created by a washed out irrigation ditch, swimming pools. On point after point, the answer has been very clear: no, there is no expansion of authority, there is no new permitting requirement. There is no ''there'' there. There is just partisan hysteria with no basis in fact.

And yet, here we are today, once again, having a hearing on the scope of this proposed clean water rule with the same tired discredited arguments, conspiracy theories that this draft rule is some type of an expansion of jurisdiction. If we are going to have an honest discussion on this subject, I think we need to start by acknowledging that the draft rule is not an expansion of the Clean Water Act authority. It is just not.

Now, I have visited with ranchers and landowners from my district. I understand there have been some anxieties about what this rulemaking means. Some have actually sought to foment some of that fear and anxiety. And when the draft rule was released last year, I agreed that there could be some additional specificity in a few areas before the final rule was released. It is understandable on a complex, complicated subject, that there might be some areas that need clarity.

The Administration has responded. They have responded to these points saying, time and again, they would evaluate comments, make changes in the final rule to provide more specific definition, to provide more clarity, clearer designations for tributaries, assurances that the current exemptions for agriculture are going to stay on the books. That is why we have a public comment process, and it seems to be working.

On the Forest Service Groundwater Directive, Mr. Chair, the Forest Service has put that directive on hold. But it is worth noting that Congress has directed the Forest Service in numerous laws to help manage and protect groundwater resources on national forest land. So it is an issue that needs attention. But right now it seems to me that it is really rather moot.

When we are done with this exercise, Mr. Chair, I do hope that we can get back to trying to work together to solve real problems that are within the jurisdiction of this committee. There are many of them that need our attention, and I will look forward to the time when we can do that together.

I yield back. Thank you.

Dr. FLEMING. The gentleman yields back.

We will now hear from our witnesses. Each witness' written testimony will appear in full in the hearing record, so I ask that witnesses keep their oral statement to 5 minutes, as outlined in our invitation letter to you under Committee Rule 4(a).

I will explain the timing lights very simply. You have 5 minutes. You will be under the green light for the first 4. Then it turns yellow, and then, at the end of that 1 minute, when it turns red, we need for you to immediately conclude so that we can hear everybody's testimony and get to questions.

I would also like to note, in addition to the witnesses we have today, we have Mr. Estevan Lopez, the Commissioner of the Bureau of Reclamation, who was also invited to testify at today's hearing. As I indicated in my opening statement, the Bureau has refused for the second year in a row to provide a witness to answer any questions stemming from written testimony. That vacancy speaks volumes of the Administration's defense of its proposal.

That said, I now recognize Mr. James Ogsbury, Executive Director of the Western Governors' Association, based in Denver, Colorado, to testify.

STATEMENT OF JAMES OGSBURY, EXECUTIVE DIRECTOR, WESTERN GOVERNORS' ASSOCIATION, DENVER, COLORADO

Mr. OGSBURY. Thank you, Chairman Fleming, Ranking Member Huffman, and members of the subcommittee. My name is Jim Ogsbury, and I am the Executive Director of the Western Governors' Association. WGA is an independent, non-partisan organization representing 19 Western Governors and 3 U.S. flag islands. I appreciate this opportunity to share the perspective of Western Governors on recent Federal water-related regulatory proposals.

The Western Governors have adopted a policy resolution that directly speaks to water resource management. The resolution states, ''States are the primary authority for allocating, administering, protecting, and developing water resources, and they are primarily responsible for water supply planning within their boundaries. States have the ultimate say in the management of their water resources, and are best suited to speak to the unique nature of Western water law and hydrology.''

The Governors' resolution is based on the prior appropriation doctrine, the foundation of Western water law, under which states are the authority to issue rights for water use. State authority should be the starting point of any Federal regulatory action on water.

In recent years, however, several regulatory proposals have inadequately recognized this principle. Whatever the issue at hand, WGA's position on Federal water regulation is the same: agencies must recognize state authority in water management. Again, quoting from the Governors' policy resolution, ''nothing in any regulatory action should be construed as intending to affect states' primacy over the allocation and administration of their water resources.''

This articulates the Governors' principal concern about the Federal actions being discussed today. They inadequately recognize the fact that states have the authority and the competency to manage water resources.

With respect to the Forest Service's proposed directive on groundwater resource management, the Western Governors identified several concerns with the directive, and requested meaningful consultation with the states. I am pleased to report that the Service has informed me that it has suspended work on the directive all together, and has assured me that the agency will work more closely and meaningfully with states in the future. We applaud this development and this commitment.

In the meantime, I would emphasize that states do possess sole and exclusive management authority for groundwater. This authority has been recognized by Congress and upheld by the U.S. Supreme Court. Congress has created limited Federal Reserve rights to surface water, but no Federal statute or Federal appellate court has ever extended those rights to groundwater. Western Governors differ regarding the substance of the draft Waters of the

United States rule issued by the EPA and the Army Corps of Engineers.

All Western Governors, however, recognize the primacy of state authority over water resources within state boundaries. And the WGA is concerned that the rulemaking process did not involve meaningful consultation with the states during the draft rule's development. Western Governors continue to appeal to Federal agencies to be treated as authentic partners at the earliest stages of rulemaking, and throughout the process, because of the potential impact of these rules on state authority.

On this point it is worth noting that the EPA Science Advisory Board panel for the review of the agency's water body connectivity report—purportedly the scientific basis for the rule—included no state representation. The report was developed without, therefore, the regulatory experience, scientific resources, and on-the-ground knowledge possessed by state water professionals.

In conclusion, state authority is the cornerstone of effective water management in the West. This is not simply a matter of precedent or legal authority; states are best situated to understand their own unique legal frameworks, local hydrology, and citizen needs. Congress and the Supreme Court have a long-standing tradition of deference to state water law, and state authority over the resource. Western Governors are honored to work with the subcommittee to maintain that rich tradition. Thank you.

[The prepared statement of Mr. Ogsbury follows:]

PREPARED STATEMENT OF JAMES D. OGSBURY, EXECUTIVE DIRECTOR, WESTERN GOVERNORS' ASSOCIATION

Mr. Chairman and members of the subcommittee, I sincerely appreciate your invitation to testify today on behalf of the Western Governors' Association (WGA). My name is James D. Ogsbury and I am the Association's Executive Director. WGA is an independent, non-partisan organization representing the Governors of 19 western states and 3 U.S.-flag islands. I am honored to share with the subcommittee the perspective of the Western Governors regarding recent Federal water-related regulatory proposals.

Water is a precious resource everywhere but especially in the West, where arid conditions—currently exacerbated by drought in many states—mean that water is particularly prized. Water is different in the West: our hydrology and legal structures governing water rights and usage are distinct from other parts of the Nation.

The Western Governors have a policy resolution that directly speaks to water resource management.[1] In that resolution, the Governors reiterate a fact recognized by both Congress and the U.S. Supreme Court:

> States are the primary authority for allocating, administering, protecting and developing water resources, and they are primarily responsible for water supply planning within their boundaries. States have the ultimate say in the management of their water resources and are best suited to speak to the unique nature of western water law and hydrology.

The Governors' statement is the basis of all of WGA's work on water. The resolution is based on the prior appropriation doctrine, the foundation of western water law under which states are the authority to issue rights for water use. The premises of prior appropriation and state authority should be the starting point of any Federal regulatory action on water as well. In recent years, however, several regulatory proposals from the Federal agencies have inadequately recognized state authority.

I will share perspectives from the Governors on each of the proposed regulatory directives and rules under consideration today, but my primary point will be the

---

[1] Western Governors' Association. Policy Resolution 2014–03, *Water Resource Management in the West.* 2014. http://www.westgov.org/policies/301-water/597-water-resource-management-in-the-west-resolution-wga.

same for all three issues: Federal agencies must recognize state authority in water management. Again quoting from the Governors' policy resolution, "nothing in any . . . regulatory action should be construed as . . . intending to affect states' primacy over the allocation and administration of their water resources." Therein lies the key concern underlying all of the pending Federal regulations relating to water: they inadequately recognize the simple fact that states have the authority and competency to manage water resources.

GROUNDWATER

In formal comments to the U.S. Forest Service (Forest Service or USFS) regarding the agency's proposed directive on groundwater resource management, the Western Governors identified several concerns with the directive and requested meaningful consultation with the states. I am pleased to tell you that the Forest Service is, indeed, engaging in an active conversation with western water resource managers at this time. WGA applauds that effort. I hope that the discussions occurring now will serve as a model for Federal-state consultation before proposals are issued in the future.

If the Forest Service issues a revised groundwater proposal, WGA urges the agency to fully recognize and defer to the states' management authority. As the Governors stated in their formal comments to USFS, the proposed directive could be construed to assert USFS ownership of state groundwater through use of the phrase "National Forest System (NFS) groundwater resources" throughout the document.[2] This vague and insufficient acknowledgement of the states' authority over groundwater is also evident in the stated objective of the proposed directive, which is to "manage groundwater underlying NFS lands cooperatively with states."[3] This language misleadingly suggests that the USFS has equal authority with the states over groundwater management, which it does not.[4]

The Governors also expressed concern that the proposed directive would lead USFS employees to make decisions regarding special use permits based on the amount of water withdrawn with a state issued water right; that is, a quantity that the state has already authorized for diversion and depletion.[5] The proposal calls on USFS employees to consider the effects of proposed actions on groundwater quantity and to require conservation strategies to limit total water withdrawals before issuing special use authorizations. While these provisions are surely well-intentioned, they ignore the fundamental concept of the states' authority to determine how much groundwater can be withdrawn within their boundaries.

Moreover, the proposed directive instructs employees to assume that surface water and groundwater are hydraulically connected, regardless of whether state law treats these resources separately.[6] Not only does this disregard individual states' law, it also creates potential for misinterpretation of the directive to mean that the USFS holds management authority for both groundwater and, by extension, the surface water to which it assumes to be hydraulically connected.

The Forest Service has been made well aware of these concerns through comments from the Western Governors' Association, the Western States Water Council—an organization for state water managers—and through individual comments from states. The agency has responded with an offer to discuss our concerns and is currently engaged in such discussions with members of the Western States Water Council. WGA encourages that dialog to proceed and we hope that if a re-

---

[2] Western Governors' Association. "Comments on FS–2014–0001—Proposed Directive on Groundwater Resource Management, Forest Service Manual 2560." Formal comments to USDA Forest Service. 2 Oct. 2014. http://www.westgov.org/letters-testimony/342-water/803-comments-usfs-groundwater-proposed-directive.

[3] Proposed Directive on Groundwater Resource Management, Forest Service Manual 2560. 79 FR 25815. 6 May 2014. See Section 2560.02–01 of draft available from U.S. Forest Service, http://www.fs.fed.us/geology/groundwater.html.

[4] The proposed directive on groundwater references Forest Service Manual 2540 (FSM) which claims that "'groundwater as well as surface water is included" in the Federal reserved water rights recognized in *Winters* v. *U.S.*, 207 U.S. 564 (1908) (FSM 2541.01, September 4, 2007). The *Winters* doctrine acknowledges Federal reserved rights to water to secure adequate flows (as required by the Organic Act), but *Winters* has never been recognized as applicable to groundwater by any Federal appellate court. The Forest Service Manual language regarding groundwater was never available for public comment and thus was never challenged in a formal comment period.

[5] Proposed Directive on Groundwater Resource Management, Forest Service Manual 2560. 79 FR 25815. 6 May 2014. See Sections 2560.03–4–a, 2561–2, and 2562.1–3 of draft available from U.S. Forest Service, http://www.fs.fed.us/geology/groundwater.html.

[6] Proposed Directive on Groundwater Resource Management, Forest Service Manual 2560. 79 FR 25815. 6 May 2014. See Sections 2560.03–2 and 2561.1 of draft available from U.S. Forest Service, http://www.fs.fed.us/geology/groundwater.html.

vised directive is issued, that state authority will serve as the cornerstone of the document.

Despite these productive conversations, WGA believes it is important to reiterate the point that states are the sole management authority for groundwater. In 2012, Federal trustees asserted claims for damages to groundwater in a natural resource damage case in New Mexico.[7] This action was unprecedented, as the Federal Government does not inherently own groundwater to damage. Congress has created Federal reserved rights to surface water, but no Federal statute or Federal appellate court has extended those rights to groundwater. The Federal trustees' legal position thus challenged the western states' exclusive management of the groundwater resources within their respective boundaries.

These damage claims demonstrate a history of Federal attempts to lay claim to a resource that Congress has recognized—and the Supreme Court has affirmed—belongs to the states. It is because of this history that I believe it is important to speak to you today on behalf of the Western Governors. While I am hopeful about the outlook for a productive relationship with the USFS on the groundwater directive, other issues remain—and continue to arise—that would challenge state authority over water resources. I ask the subcommittee to help the Western Governors protect this long-standing authority.

SKI AREA WATER RIGHTS

Another proposal from the Forest Service that could be construed as challenging state authority is a proposed addition to the agency's employee handbook regarding ski area water rights. As the Governors stated in their formal comments on the proposal, some language within the proposed ski area directive appears to be an effort by USFS to utilize special use authorization as a means to manage water use and water rights on NFS lands.[8] Any such effort must be consistent with underlying state law regarding the acquisition and transfer of water rights.

Certain terms within the proposed directive are undefined, creating ambiguity for states and permittees. For instance, the clause requires water right holders to obtain advance written approval from the USFS before water rights can be divided, transferred, or modified if such action will "adversely affect" the availability of those rights to support operation of the ski area.[9] The term "adversely affect" is not defined, nor does the paragraph explain who makes this determination. Regardless of its precise meaning, the overall intent of the directive is apparent: to add a layer of Federal regulatory oversight to state-managed water right systems on NFS lands.

WATERS OF THE UNITED STATES

While the proposed rule from the Environmental Protection Agency (EPA) and Army Corps of Engineers (Corps) to redefine the jurisdiction of the Clean Water Act (CWA) is meant to clarify the scope of the regulation, the current proposal has, instead, created new points of ambiguity. One point lacking clarity is the matter of connectivity. The proposed rule would allow "shallow subsurface flow connection"—a term it does not define—to establish jurisdiction between surface waters. While groundwater itself is not included in the rule, the document needs measures to reiterate that groundwater is indeed solely the purview of the states.

As the Western States Water Council noted in its comments on the proposed rule, the preamble of the document explicitly states that "nothing . . . would cause the shallow subsurface connections themselves to become jurisdictional."[10] However, the

---

[7] The Chevron Questa Mine site (formerly known as the Molycorp, Inc. site) is undergoing remediation per the Comprehensive Environmental Response, Compensation, and Liability Act. The Western Governors' Association issued a letter expressing concerns about the trustees' claims on May 25, 2012. Twelve members of the Council of Western Attorneys General also issued a letter dated March 7, 2012. Both letters are available from WGA staff.

[8] Western Governors' Association. "Comments on FS—FRDOC—0001–1886—Ski Area Water Rights on NFS Lands." Formal comments to USDA Forest Service. 21 Aug. 2014. http://www.westgov.org/letters-testimony/299-letters-testimony-2014/774-comments-wga-weighs-in-on-forest-service-ski-area-water-rights.

[9] Proposed directive on Ski Area Water Rights on National Forest System Lands. 79 FR 35513. 23 June 2014. See paragraph F–4–b of draft available from U.S. Forest Service, http://www.fs.fed.us/specialuses/.

[10] Western States Water Council. "Attention—Docket ID No. EPA–HQ–OW–2011–0880" (Definition of 'Waters of the United States' Under the Clean Water Act). Formal comments to the Environmental Protection Agency (EPA) and the U.S. Army Corps of Engineers (Corps). 15 Oct. 2014. http://www.westernstateswater.org/wp-content/uploads/2012/10/Combined-CWA-WOTUS-Rule-Document-Final-101514.pdf. These comments were incorporated by reference into the Western Governors' Association's comments. The comments reference: Definition of "Waters of

preamble will not be published once the rule is codified. Without this clarifying statement, confusion could arise regarding the jurisdictional status of subsurface water.

Furthermore, the EPA's Scientific Advisory Board report on the connectivity of water indicated support for using connectivity as a scientific basis for even broader CWA jurisdiction than what is now suggested under the proposed rule. Though that recommendation will not necessarily change the content of the final rule, the implications are troubling. Legal authority and precedent are at the core of the question of Federal jurisdiction under the CWA. Both laws and hydrology vary from state to state. As the Governors stated in their formal comments on the proposed rule, the best policy when considering the intersection of science and law is one that allows for regional flexibility and acknowledges the role of state experts who live with—and intimately understand—the issue at hand.[11]

It is worth noting that the SAB panel for the review of the EPA water body connectivity report included no state representatives.[12] The report was therefore developed without the regulatory expertise, scientific resources and on-the-ground knowledge possessed by state professionals. EPA inadequately recognized the role of the states in forming its SAB panel. Likewise, the agency's reasoning that its proposed rule is needed to ensure protection of waters that we all value inadequately recognizes the role of the states in ensuring water quality.

CONCLUSION

State authority is the cornerstone of effective water management in the West. This is not simply a matter of precedent; states are best situated to understand their own unique legal frameworks, local hydrology and citizen needs. Federal efforts to assume greater authority over water jeopardize the distinct advantages of having on-the-ground resource management.

Even though legal precedent is not the only justification for state water management, it is one of the most powerful mechanisms Governors have to maintain their authority. Congress and the Supreme Court are squarely on the side of the states. That management authority is something that Western Governors intend to fight for vehemently and vocally. We welcome the opportunity to partner with the subcommittee to maintain the states' authority on water.

QUESTIONS SUBMITTED FOR THE RECORD BY THE HON. DAN NEWHOUSE TO JAMES OGSBURY, WESTERN GOVERNORS' ASSOCIATION

Question 1. Is it true that the states have authority to determine how much groundwater can be withdrawn within their boundaries?

Answer. Yes. The U.S. Supreme Court held in *California Oregon Power Co. v. Beaver Portland Cement Co.*, 295 U.S. 142 (1935), that states have exclusive authority over groundwater, finding that following the Desert Land Act of 1877 ". . . all non-navigable waters then a part of the public domain became *publici juris*, subject to the plenary control of the designated states. . . ."

Question 2. When it comes to surface water withdrawals on some Federal lands, the Federal Government can have reserved water rights on these withdrawals. Does the Federal Government have reserved water rights on groundwater?

Answer. No. Certain Federal agencies have reserved water rights provided by the Organic Administration Act of 1897 and affirmed by the U.S. Supreme Court in *Winters* v. *U.S.*, 207 U.S. 564 (1908). The reserved rights recognized in the *Winters* doctrine have never been recognized as applicable to groundwater by Congress or any Federal appellate court.

---

the United States'' Under the Clean Water Act. 79 FR 22269, pg. 22210. 21 Apr. 2014 (to be codified at 40 CFR Part 230.3).

[11] Western Governors' Association. "Comments on Docket ID No. EPA–HQ–OW–2011–0880—Definition of 'Waters of the United States' Under the Clean Water Act." Formal comments to EPA and the Corps. 14 Nov. 2014. http://www.westgov.org/letters-testimony/342-water/837-comments-Governors-submit-comments-on-definition-of-waters-of-the-united-states-under-the-clean-water-act.

[12] EPA. "Members of the Panel for the Review of the EPA Water Body Connectivity Report." Accessed 17 Oct. 2014. http://yosemite.epa.gov/sab/sabpeople.nsf/WebExternalSubCommittee Rosters?OpenView&committee=BOARD&subcommittee=Panel%20for%20the%20Review%20of%20the%20EPA%20Water%20Body%20Connectivity%20Report.

Question 3. Does the Forest Service Groundwater Directive give more power to the Federal Government on groundwater at the expense of states? What will be the impact of this change?

Answer. As the Governors stated in their formal comments to USFS, the proposed directive could be construed to assert USFS ownership of state groundwater through use of the phrase "National Forest System (NFS) groundwater resources" throughout the document.[1] This vague and insufficient acknowledgement of the states' authority over groundwater is also evident in the stated objective of the proposed directive, which is to "manage groundwater underlying NFS lands cooperatively with states."[2] This language misleadingly suggests that the USFS has equal authority with the states over groundwater management, which it does not. Because of differences in state laws, the unique hydrological characteristics of states and other considerations, states continue to be the appropriate entity to manage groundwater resources.

The Western Governors' Association is pleased that the U.S. Forest Service has stopped its work on the proposed directive regarding groundwater resource management, which will help avoid unforeseen impacts.

———

Dr. FLEMING. Thank you, Mr. Ogsbury.

Next we have the Honorable Ron Sullivan, an elected board member of the Eastern Municipal Water District in Perris, California.

You are recognized for 5 minutes, sir.

STATEMENT OF RON SULLIVAN, BOARD OF DIRECTORS, DIVISION 4, EASTERN MUNICIPAL WATER DISTRICT, PERRIS, CALIFORNIA

Mr. SULLIVAN. Thank you, Mr. Chairman, Chairman Fleming, and Ranking Member Huffman from California, members of the subcommittee. We thank you for the opportunity to testify today. My name is Ron Sullivan, and I am speaking today on behalf of the National Water Resources Association.

The NWRA members are the people who deliver safe drinking water and irrigation water, and we ensure that the objectives of the Clean Water Act are met on a daily basis. I have served 12 years on the board of Eastern Municipal Water District in Riverside County, California. We are a leader in efficient water management, most particularly reuse and reclamation of water, also known as water recycling.

Providing water services in my district requires a regular engagement of at least 28 Federal, state, and local agencies. Water travels a long pipeline of government regulation before it comes out of the tap or is returned to a river or, in our case, is recycled for beneficial use. We support the goals of the Clean Water Act. However, the proposed rule to redefine "Waters of the U.S." is problematic. It will make it harder for places like my home state of California to meet the water needs and deal with the drought as it currently exists.

The subcommittee should be particularly concerned with the potential impacts of this rule on water delivery systems operated by

[1] Western Governors' Association. "Comments on FS–2014–0001—Proposed Directive on Groundwater Resource Management, Forest Service Manual 2560." Formal comments to USDA Forest Service. 2 Oct. 2014. http://www.westgov.org/letters-testimony/342-water/803-comments-usfs-groundwater-proposed-directive.

[2] Proposed Directive on Groundwater Resource Management, Forest Service Manual 2560. 79 FR 25815. 6 May 2014. See Section 2560.02–01 of draft available from U.S. Forest Service. http://www.fs.fed.us/geology/groundwater.html.

the Bureau of Reclamation and its customers. The current drought has emphasized the importance of water supply. The Administration's national climate assessment in 2014 declared—''Climate changes pose challenges for an already parched region that is expected to get hotter and, in its southern half, significantly drier. Increased heat and changes to rain and snow pack will send ripple effects throughout the region's critical agricultural section, affecting the lives and economies of approximately 15 million.''

NWRA shares this concern, but we are worried that the proposed rule will make it more difficult to meet the water needs and challenges proposed by the changing climate. Recycled water is an environmentally friendly method to utilize local water resources. Water recycling storage and conveyance facilities are frequently located in a flood plain or otherwise adjacent to jurisdictional water, where all waters would be categorically defined as ''Waters of the U.S.'' The proposed rule's wastewater treatment exemption would not extend to an associated water recycling facility, because such facilities are not expressly designed to meet the requirements of the Clean Water Act, a condition stipulated in the rule.

California has established a statewide goal of recycling 2.5 million acre-feet of water by 2030. In the year 2000, we attained about 25 percent of that, which is going to make the remaining part of it very difficult to get 2.5 million acre-feet, especially if the permitting on this rule would take some of these districts another 3 to 8 years to get through the process.

The proposed rule impact on recycled water projects can be illustrated in my own water district. At Eastern Municipal Water District, we utilize 100 percent of the recycled water that we generate in all four of our plants. Recycled water constitutes 30 percent of our entire water supply portfolio, over 38,000 acre-feet annually. And this is a year-in, year-out, day-in, day-out flow that we can always depend on.

We are concerned that, under the proposed rule, 10 of Eastern Municipal Water District's recycled storage facilities could become jurisdictional, because they are located in flood plains, or adjacent to jurisdictional waters, and may possess a subsurface hydrologic connection to a jurisdictional water. After becoming jurisdictional, regular maintenance and vegetation removal of these 500 acres of ponds would require an additional 404 permit, as well as a Section 401 permit. This added regulatory burden could hamper us in the development of this drought-proof water supply that we so dearly depend on.

We are concerned with the Forest Service. We know that it has been put on the table a little bit. But we did have our concerns because we do have water rights out of the flow that comes out of the national forest, and it is of deep concern to us, because it is highly potable water, and it is terrific water. Thank you.

[The prepared statement of Mr. Sullivan follows:]

PREPARED STATEMENT OF RONALD SULLIVAN, EASTERN MUNICIPAL WATER DISTRICT, ON BEHALF OF NATIONAL WATER RESOURCES ASSOCIATION

Mr. Chairman, Ranking Member Huffman, members of the committee, thank you for this opportunity to testify today regarding the impact that Federal actions have on water and power users and landowners. My name is Ron Sullivan, and I am speaking today on behalf of the National Water Resources Association. NWRA members are agricultural and municipal water providers, state associations, and individuals dedicated to the conservation, enhancement and efficient management of water. We are the people who deliver safe drinking water and irrigation water, and we ensure that the objectives of the Clean Water Act are met.

I have served 12 years on the board of Eastern Municipal Water District ("Eastern MWD") in Riverside County, California. My District provides water and wastewater services to 785,000 people in the growing Inland Empire. We are a leader in efficient water management, most particularly reuse and reclamation of water, also known as water recycling, where we are considered industry leaders. Providing water services in my District requires the regular engagement of at least 8 Federal agencies, 5 state agencies, several county agencies, and at least 15 municipal agencies. Water travels a long pipeline of government regulation before it comes out of the tap or is returned to a river—or in our case, is recycled for beneficial use.

The Federal Government plays a significant but not the only role in ensuring an adequate and safe supply of water. In fact, in Eastern MWD's case, the Federal Government's contribution to funding water infrastructure for supply, treatment, and environmental benefits is minuscule, at less than 2 percent of the capital investment we make in people and habitats. Yet Federal agencies too often act as if they alone are charged with managing resources and protecting public interest in water.

I and my fellow board members, the public officials who treat and serve water, and the elected and appointed public servants who manage water resources across the country have all taken oaths to protect the public and its investment in water. We are partners with the Federal Government in providing this essential public service, and we need to be integrated into the decisionmaking process for policies that affect our mandate. When that process short-circuits local and state government involvement, the public suffers cost increases, bureaucratic delays, and ultimately a degraded, less efficient level of service to the public. This subcommittee has a degree of jurisdiction over two recent examples of the breakdown between Federal and local engagement:

WATERS OF THE UNITED STATES

The first of these examples is the proposed rule published by the U.S. Environmental Protection Agency and the U.S. Army Corps of Engineers last April to redefine "Waters of the U.S." that are subject to the Clean Water Act. The rule was recently referred to the Office of Management and Budget for final review, after the agencies sifted through more than one million public comments. I understand that most comments from public agencies expressed opposition to the rule, citing concerns about the proposed rule's impact on storm water, waste water and recycled water facilities, conveyance ditches, and water delivery systems. Under the agencies' proposal, jurisdiction of the rule would be expanded to include all waters, not just wetlands, adjacent to traditional navigable waters and undefined riparian areas and floodplains. Without a clear definition for a "significant" nexus to traditional navigable waters, ephemeral and intermittent streams would be considered categorically jurisdictional. During numerous congressional hearings with administration officials, it became clear that Federal regulators failed to adequately confer with and accommodate concerns raised by state and local governments. NWRA is concerned that the proposed rule misses the mark. As drafted it does not provide the additional clarity and certainty that water users and others have asked for and will make meeting current and future water supply needs more difficult. In fact, we are concerned that the cost of compliance will far out-weigh any marginal benefit in water quality.

This subcommittee should be particularly concerned with the potential impacts of this rule on water delivery systems owned and operated by the Bureau of Reclamation. Water delivery systems in the 17 Reclamation states will be subject to new permitting requirements and additional infrastructure costs as these facilities are redefined as waters of the United States. Certainly the current drought across much of the West has emphasized the importance of water storage and delivery and the need to maintain the capacity and operating efficiency and flexibility of these systems. The Administration's own National Climate Assessment in 2014 declared:

> The Southwest is the hottest and driest region of the United States, where the availability of water has defined its landscapes, history of human settlement, and modern economy. Climate changes pose challenges for an already parched region that is expected to get hotter and, in its southern half, significantly drier. Increased heat and changes to rain and snowpack will send ripple effects throughout the region's critical agriculture sector, affecting

the lives and economies of 56 million people—a population that is expected to increase 68 percent by 2050, to 94 million. Severe and sustained drought will stress water sources, already over-utilized in many areas, forcing increasing competition among farmers, energy producers, urban dwellers, and plant and animal life for the region's most precious resource.

The Administration is correct to express concern about meeting water supply needs in coming decades. NWRA shares this concern. However, we are genuinely concerned that the proposed rule will make it more difficult to meet water needs. We strongly support the Clean Water Act and the need for a rule that clarifies jurisdiction of the Act. We do not support this proposed rule and ask that Congress take action to ensure a more inclusive rulemaking process.

In order to meet water supply and wastewater treatment needs, as well as storm water control requirements, municipal utilities and irrigation districts must make substantial infrastructure investments, often requiring creative and innovative approaches. These investments will include new or expanded storage reservoirs; water reuse facilities, desalinization plants; water collection, delivery, and distribution pipelines; pump-back projects; groundwater recharge facilities; and reverse osmosis water treatment plants. Many of these facilities will, of necessity, be in close proximity to traditional navigable waters, in a riparian area or floodplain, and include features that meet the definition of a ditch, tributary or wetland. Any one of those conditions would subject the entire system or elements thereof to higher regulatory requirements, additional bureaucratic review, and much greater cost.

As the demand for water continues to rise, NWRA's members are committed to undertaking a variety of innovative efforts to meet this need. These efforts include extensive water conservation as well as water recycling. Recycled water, which is generated from the treatment and purification of wastewater, is a safe, effective and environmentally friendly method to fully utilize local water resources, and reduces the demand for imported water in the arid Southwest. The processes and infrastructure to treat, store and distribute recycled water are costly, but are becoming increasingly feasible in areas of the country where groundwater and surface water sources are strained and the cost or availability of imported water is prohibitive.

Water authorities across the country are investing billions of dollars in infrastructure to utilize this drought-proof water resource. My water district alone has made $188 million in capital investments in its recycled water system, and has $154 million of recycled water investments planned over the next 5 years. Treatment and distribution costs of recycled water are already high, making this valuable resource marginally cost-effective in some places. Any significant increase in regulation will escalate the cost of utilizing this water and discourage its further development.

Under the proposed rule, water reclamation and reuse facilities are not exempt from being designated "Waters of the U.S." Further, ditches that transport effluent or discharged water could also be considered a "tributary" under the proposed rule and could be categorically regulated. The proposed rule defines as a "tributary" any natural or man-made feature that has a bed, bank, ordinary high water mark, and conducts flow to another water. In addition, water recycling storage and conveyance facilities are frequently located in a floodplain or otherwise adjacent to jurisdictional water where all waters are categorically defined as "Waters of the U.S." While the proposed rule includes an exemption for artificial lakes and ponds used exclusively for settling basins, such reuse facilities can function or take on the characteristics of a wetland and can receive and discharge water into surface ditches that are not exempt. The proposed rule's wastewater treatment exemption would not extend to an associated water recycling facility because such facilities are not expressly "designed to meet the requirements of the Clean Water Act;" a condition stipulated in the rule. Many states have acknowledged the value of recycled water. Some states like California have established a statewide goal (California Water Plan) of recycling 2.5 million acre feet (MAF) of water by 2030. In 2009, 0.67 MAF was recycled; increasing to 2.5 MAF is ambitious, but necessary to help drought-proof the state. Currently 3.5 MAF of treated wastewater is being discharged to the ocean, and not beneficially reused.

The proposed rule's impact on recycled water projects can be illustrated in my own water district. Eastern MWD is a water and wastewater agency that utilizes 100 percent of the recycled water it generates, with recycled water constituting 30 percent of our entire water supply portfolio—over 38,000 acre feet annually. This critical supply is used for municipal irrigation and industrial uses, and is also used to irrigate over 10,800 acres of production agriculture in our service area. In recent years, EMWD in cooperation with Federal partners at the Bureau of Reclamation, has developed 5,714 acre-feet of seasonal storage ponds, 16 million gallons of elevated storage tanks (to pressurize the system), over 200 miles of recycled distribution water pipelines, and 19 pumping facilities. EMWD currently has greater demand than supply for recycled water, and in response has prepared unique allocations for customers.

We are concerned that under the proposed rule, 10 EMWD recycled water storage sites could become jurisdictional because they are located in floodplains, are adjacent to jurisdictional waters, and may possess a subsurface hydrologic connection to jurisdictional waters. After becoming jurisdictional, regular maintenance and vegetation removal of these 500 acres of ponds would require Section 404 Army Corps of Engineers permits as well as Section 401 water quality permits from the state. This added regulatory burden would not only increase the cost of recycled water, and potentially delay further development of recycled water storage ponds, but could hamper the development of this drought-proof water supply. Numerous agencies in the arid Southwest share this scenario, concern, and dilemma.

Despite verbal assurances that the rule with not regulate groundwater, we also remain concerned that groundwater banking and recharge projects will be enveloped by this rule. Multiple NWRA members operate groundwater banking and recharge projects to capture and store unused irrigation water and treated effluent from municipal treatment plants. Some of these shallow banking aquifers are adjacent to rivers. The agencies should provide additional clarity in the rule that groundwater, shallow subsurface aquifers, and groundwater banking and recharge projects will not be considered waters of the United States.

My testimony is largely focused on municipal water supplier concerns, and I understand that other witnesses will discuss agricultural water user perspectives in depth. However, it is vital I note that the proposed ''Waters of the United States'' rule is also very concerning to NWRA's agricultural water providers. The proposed rule would largely capture irrigation features that are currently not jurisdictional. Last week Administrator McCarthy stated in a blog post that the EPA would address these concern in the revised rule. This statement encourages us. However, we are not wholly confident that agricultural concerns will be addressed because similar assertions about protecting agriculture were made when the rule was unveiled last April.

In summary, we need Congress to act on this proposed rule. The scope of the proposed rule is so broad and its potential impacts are so great, that we cannot entrust the Federal agencies to address all the concerns that have been raised with this rule. And Congress cannot wait and hope that reason will prevail in a final rule. Under the Clean Water Act, water managers are civilly and criminally liable for violations, and any citizen can file suit for a perceived non-compliance. We are vulnerable to litigation the very day this rule is finalized. NWRA members would prefer to invest public funds in infrastructure and environmental enhancement rather than litigation. Legislation that mandates intergovernmental and stakeholder involvement in defining waters of the United States will do far more to protect the public and the environment and provide certainty to water managers and users.

FOREST SERVICE GROUNDWATER MANAGEMENT DIRECTIVE

The second example of the breakdown between Federal and local agency engagement is the Forest Service's Proposed Directive on Groundwater Resource Management. This is deeply concerning to many of NWRA's members because it creates a great deal of uncertainty about the management and use of groundwater. With limited exception Congress and the Courts have largely relegated groundwater management authorities to the states. The Groundwater Directive creates a number of concerns from a state's rights perspective and from a practical management perspective. Our fundamental concern is that the Forest Service does not have the statutory authority to establish a groundwater directive. However, as an on-the-ground water provider, I will focus my comments today on the practical challenges and uncertainties that this proposal would create from a water supply perspective.

Eastern MWD is designated by the state of California as the Monitoring Entity to collect and report regional groundwater data throughout the California Statewide Groundwater Elevation Monitoring program. The agency also has existing water rights and water supply components that are adjacent to, or downstream from, Forest Service lands. As a result, Eastern MWD is uniquely positioned to provide insight as both a regional agency engaged by the state in aspects of groundwater management, and as a water provider with resources that could be directly affected by the proposed groundwater directive.

Like many water providers, Eastern MWD manages a broad portfolio of water supply resources to meet municipal, industrial and agricultural demands. As previously noted, we utilize surface water supplies, recycled water supplies and groundwater supplies. In relation to groundwater, Eastern MWD has several important components that could be significantly affected by the Forest Service Groundwater Directive. We accrue a water supply credit for groundwater that seeps into the San Jacinto Tunnel, which is a regional water transmission facility that brings imported water into our region. The construction of the San Jacinto Tunnel intercepted a local aquifer in which groundwater seeped. Eastern MWD had been pumping this groundwater and as a result, negotiated an agreement with the Tunnel owner to provide a credit for this seepage. This water is important because Eastern MWD is currently credited for the roughly 4,588 acre feet of tunnel seepage water annually. However, because the Tunnel is in the proximity of Forest Service land, we are concerned that the proposed groundwater directive could create an avenue for the Federal Government, through the Forest Service, to make a claim against this water supply. Additionally, Eastern MWD has water rights in the San Jacinto River watershed which begins in Forest Service land. We are concerned that the proposed groundwater directive would not only limit our ability to manage this resource, but could adversely affect our water rights.

The nature of groundwater varies significantly from one region of the country to another. Water rights and legal agreements affecting surface and groundwater can be complicated. The proposed directive fails to recognize the nuances of geography and existing agreements and instead provides blank assumptions that may be detrimental to many long-standing water rights holders.

We are seeking assurances from the Forest Service that western water rights and management abilities will not be limited by this proposal. NWRA's concerns are significant enough that it has requested a withdrawal of this ambiguous and far-reaching proposal. We understand that the Forest Service has pulled back from this proposal and has indicated that they will try to address state and water user concerns. As with explanations provided by the Federal agency regarding our concerns with the Clean Water Act rule, we are heartened by this news, but remain concerned that agency objectives might short-change consultations with state and local governments. We also want to emphasize that the Forest Service needs to improve its outreach efforts to stakeholders. Prior to issuing this directive, the Forest Service failed to reach out to either water users or the states.

Respecting the role of states in water management and respecting state allocated water rights is fundamental to meeting current and future water needs. Any future proposal needs to consider these facts and ensure that water rights and the role of states are clearly protected.

CONCLUSION

Again, I would like to thank the committee for holding this hearing and inviting NWRA to share its views. We have enjoyed long and constructive relationships with numerous Federal agencies responsible for water supply, management, and protection. And we fully anticipate maintaining and enhancing those relationships in the future. However, we are concerned when Federal agencies presume a disproportionate share of authority or influence, neglecting other water partners at the state and local levels. We appreciate the oversight and, when necessary, the intervention in Congress to restore balance. Thank you for accepting that responsibility. We look forward to working with you and the Federal agencies as we protect the public and its investments in water resources and infrastructure.

———

Dr. FLEMING. Thank you, Mr. Sullivan.

The Chair now recognizes Mr. Mauck, Commissioner for District 1 of Clear Creek County, Colorado, to testify.

You have 5 minutes, sir.

STATEMENT OF TIMOTHY MAUCK, COMMISSIONER, DISTRICT 1, CLEAR CREEK COUNTY, COLORADO

Mr. MAUCK. Thank you, Chairman Fleming, Ranking Member Huffman, members of the committee. My name is Timothy Mauck, Commissioner from Clear Creek County, Colorado. Thank you for this opportunity to convey how important clean water is for my community. The proposed clean water rule will protect the headwaters, tributaries, and wetlands that are essential for providing the high-quality water that supports the hunting, fishing, rafting, and outdoor recreation that are an economic backbone for my community.

Clean water from streams and wetlands also provides drinking water for thousands of our residents. Clear Creek County is truly a headwater county. We are bordered by the Continental Divide and provide clean water for downstream communities within the Denver Metropolitan Area. We face the legacy impacts of historic silver and gold mining. We have struggled with maintaining water quality due to mine runoff, and have worked consistently to treat contaminated water to reclaim abandoned mine sites.

Clear Creek has made a remarkable rebound over the past 30 years, as we have made progress, like so much of the country, toward the Clean Water Act goals of fishable and swimmable waters.

In addition, these strides in water quality, while important in their own right, have also made Clear Creek County an outdoor recreation destination. Clear Creek hosts the second-most commercial rafting trips in Colorado. White water rafting alone has a total economic impact to the community of approximately $23 million. Hunting and angling generates a total economic impact of nearly $6 million to the county. This is not only the story of Clear Creek, but also across Colorado and the Nation.

According to the National Shooting Sports Foundation, hunting and angling's total economic impact is $192 billion. Outdoor recreation in Colorado generates $13.2 billion, and employs more than 124,000 people. Across the country it generates $646 billion and 6.1 million jobs. Many of these jobs are dependent on clean water, and will benefit from the EPA and Army Corps of Engineers' efforts.

In fact, 55 percent of stream miles in the historic range of native trout in our state are intermittent or ephemeral, and would be clearly protected by the clean water rule. Even with seasonal flow, these waters provide habitat for trout, or simply maintain the water quality needed by fish in downstream rivers.

As an avid waterfowler, I have spent many cold mornings in the wetlands of sloughs and creeks feeding the South Platte, and know how important it is to protect these places from irresponsible development.

As an elected official with the responsibility of looking after our county's finances, I am concerned about undue regulatory burden. However, the rule will restore jurisdiction to fewer of the waters than had been covered from the passage of the Clean Water Act in 1972, until the first Supreme Court decision in 2001 weakened the law.

During that time period, the population of Clear Creek increased from approximately 5,900 to 9,400. Colorado's population nearly doubled from 2.2 million to 4.4 million. The state's gross domestic product increased more than tenfold, from $13.6 to $181 billion. Furthermore, natural gas production increased from 116 trillion cubic feet to 817 trillion cubic feet, and coal production increased from 5,500 short tons to 33,000 tons.

Colorado and Clear Creek County are proof that the Clean Water Act is not the barrier to growth critics would have you believe. Opponents should realize that protecting intermittent and ephemeral streams in wetlands is fully consistent with population growth, energy production, and economic development writ-large. While I understand the need for further clarity on some outstanding issues in the proposed rule, so do the EPA and Corps of Engineers.

The agencies held more than 400 stakeholder meetings, the public comment period, and received over 1 million comments— 86 percent of them were positive, in support of the proposal. And the agencies have clearly stated that this will lead to changes in the final rule. These changes should make the law clearer and more predictable for all parties, while protecting the waters that matter most.

My county is expected to grow in the future. An expansion of Interstate 70 is underway and, along with it, growth in home and road development. In addition, we face the challenge of economic diversification as we approach the end of life of the Henderson Mine, which provides a large portion of our property tax base.

There are hundreds of mine claims that exist in undeveloped or under-developed areas, many of which are very near headwater streams. The rule will help us balance the need for diversification, while providing the necessary protection for streams and wetlands as we encourage development of all kinds.

I am ready to have my county's headwaters and wetlands clearly protected under the Clean Water Act.

[The prepared statement of Mr. Mauck follows:]

PREPARED STATEMENT OF TIMOTHY MAUCK, COMMISSIONER, CLEAR CREEK COUNTY, COLORADO

My name is Timothy Mauck, a commissioner of Clear Creek County in Colorado. I was elected to the Clear Creek Board of County Commissioners in 2010 and re-elected in 2014.

Clear Creek County is a historic gold and silver mining community located in the Rocky Mountains 30 minutes west of Denver. We have a population of about 9,000 residents, and are the proud home of four 14,000 foot peaks, the Loveland Ski Area, and the Henderson Mine—North America's largest producer of primary molybdenum.

As Commissioner, I have focused on economic development, enhancing Clear Creek's recreational and tourism industries and working to bring about sensible development strategies to improve transportation along the Interstate 70 Mountain Corridor. I am passionate about hunting and angling and am an active member of Trout Unlimited and Ducks Unlimited, and a 4–H youth archery instructor.

I also serve on the boards of the Denver Regional Council of Governments, Jefferson Center for Mental Health, and as chair of the Clear Creek Greenway Authority and Clear Creek Fire Authority boards.

As an elected county commissioner, I am testifying to convey how important clean water is for my community. The proposed clean water rule will protect the headwaters, tributaries, and wetlands that are essential for providing the high quality water that supports the hunting, fishing, rafting, and outdoor recreation that are an economic backbone for my community. Clean water from streams and wetlands also provides drinking water for thousands of our residents.

Clear Creek County is truly a headwater county. We are bordered by the continental divide and provide clean water for downstream communities within the Denver Metropolitan Area. In fact, Clear Creek flows right into the Coors Brewing Company brewery in Golden, Colorado, before merging into the South Platte River which provides drinking water for Colorado residents and irrigation for our agricultural industries. We are also facing the legacy impacts of historic silver and gold mining in the area. We have struggled with maintaining water quality due to mine runoff, and have worked consistently to treat contaminated water and reclaim abandoned mine sites. I know too well the impacts of contaminated water and the costs and time it takes to mitigate and treat it. I also know Clear Creek has made a remarkable rebound over the past 30 years, as we have made progress—like so much of the country—toward the Clean Water Act goals of fishable and swimmable waters.

In addition, these strides in water quality, while important in their own right, have also made Clear Creek County an outdoor recreation destination. By river segment, Clear Creek hosts the 2nd most commercial rafting trips in Colorado, behind only the Arkansas River which is the number one rafting destination in the world. Whitewater rafting alone has a total economic impact to the community of approximately $23 million.[1] Hunting and angling generate a total economic impact of nearly $6 million to the county. This is not only the story of Clear Creek but also across Colorado and the Nation. According to the National Shooting Sports Foundation, hunting and angling's total economic impact is $192 billion.[2] Outdoor recreation in Colorado generates $13.2 billion and employs more than 124,000 people. Across the country, it generates $646 billion and 6.1 million jobs.[3] Many of these jobs are dependent on clean water, and will benefit from the EPA and Army Corps of Engineers' efforts.

In fact, 55 percent of stream miles in the historic range of native trout in our state are intermittent or ephemeral, and would clearly be protected by the clean water rule. The upper stretches of the world famous Arkansas River nearby are 68 percent intermittent or ephemeral.[4] Even with seasonal flow, these waters provide habitat for trout, or simply maintain the water quality needed by fish in downstream rivers. As a duck hunter, too, I've spent many cold mornings in the wetlands, sloughs, and creeks feeding the South Platte and know how important it is to protect these places from irresponsible development.

As an elected official with the responsibility of looking after our county's finances I am also concerned about undue regulatory burden. I have heard concerns from other county commissioners about the rule's potential for overreach. While I take their opinions very seriously, I respectfully disagree with their position. The rule will restore jurisdiction to fewer of the waters than had been covered from the passage of the Clean Water Act in 1972 until the first Supreme Court decision in 2001 weakened the law. During that time period, the population of Clear Creek County increased from approximately 5,900 to 9,400. Colorado's population nearly doubled from 2.2 million to 4.4 million.[5] The state's gross domestic product increased more than tenfold from $13.6 to $181 billion.[6] Furthermore, natural gas production increased from 116 trillion cubic feet to 817 trillion cubic feet, and coal production increased from 5,500 short tons to 33,000 tons.[7]

Colorado and Clear Creek County are proof that the Clean Water Act is not the barrier to growth critics would have you believe. If opponents of the rule are worried about returning to the previous jurisdiction of the Clean Water Act, they should realize that protecting intermittent and ephemeral streams and wetlands is fully consistent with population growth, energy production, and economic development writ-large.

Indeed, the rule should help provide more regulatory certainty and more timely review of permit applications. Currently, the need for case-by-case jurisdictional determinations on intermittent and ephemeral streams—nearly all of which are ultimately found jurisdictional—creates significant backlogs and delays. By clarifying and simplifying the question of jurisdiction for these tributaries and adjacent wetlands, applicants should be able to more quickly get the substance of their proposals reviewed without those lengthy delays created by doing case-by-case jurisdictional analyses.

Another consistent criticism of the rule has been about process. A multitude of interests have called for everything from a complete withdrawal of the rule, to a 1-year delay, to requesting another comment period. While I understand the need for further clarity on some outstanding issues, so do the EPA and Corps of Engineers. The agencies held more than 400 stakeholder meetings during the public comment period and received over 1 million comments—86 percent of them were positive in support of the proposal—and the agencies have clearly stated that this input will

---

[1] Commercial River Use in the State of Colorado: http://www.croa.org/wp-content/uploads/2015/01/2014-Commercial-Rafting-Use-Report.pdf.

[2] Hunting and Fishing: Bright Stars of the American Economy: http://www.nssf.org/PDF/research/bright%20stars%20of%20the%20economy.pdf.

[3] The Outdoor Recreation Economy: http://outdoorindustry.org/advocacy/recreation/economy.html.

[4] Waters of the United States, Colorado: http://www.tu.org/sites/default/files/colorado_wotus.pdf.

[5] U.S. Census Data: https://www.google.com/publicdata/explore?ds=kf7tgg1uo9ude_&met_y=population&idim=county:08019&hl=en&dl=en#!ctype=l&strail=false&bcs=d&nselm=h&met_y=population&scale_y=lin&ind_y=false&rdim=country&idim=county:08019&idim=state:08000&ifdim=country&hl=en_US&dl=en&ind=false.

[6] Real Gross Domestic Product By State: http://www.eia.gov/state/seds/sep_use/notes/use_gdp.pdf.

[7] State Energy Data System 1960–2012: http://www.eia.gov/state/seds/seds-data-complete.cfm?sid=CO.

lead to changes, consistent with the law and science, in the final rule. For instance, the EPA has said it never intended to give the impression the rule would regulate roadside ditches or erosional features on farm fields, and will fix those in the final rule. These changes should make the law clearer and more predictable for all parties while protecting the water that matters most.

The ongoing discussion about the Clean Water Act's jurisdiction is not a new one. We have been dealing with the impacts of unclear jurisdiction for nearly a decade and a half. We have seen a series of guidance and rulemakings, both proposed and finalized, as well as numerous court cases. The issues and positions of interested parties have been widely known for years. I fail to see how another year or even 60 days will resolve the outstanding issues for all parties. In the meantime I am ready to have my county's headwaters and wetlands clearly protected under the Clean Water Act.

I am not alone as a local elected official who supports this rule. More than 280 local elected officials signed letters in support of this rule during the comment period. Cities as large as Pittsburgh, Philadelphia, Austin, Boston and Baltimore passed resolutions or submitted comments in favor of the rule, as did counties from New Jersey to Michigan.[8] Collectively, a non-exhaustive count of the residents whose elected officials support clean water on their behalf exceeds 10 million people, a strong showing on top of the more than 800,000 supportive comments the EPA received. Those are impressive numbers to someone who represents a county of only 9,500 people, but we share their passion for protecting our waters.

Although we are small, we are expected to grow in the future. An expansion of Interstate 70 is underway, and along with it a growth in home and road development for those from nearby metropolitan areas seeking solace in the mountains. In addition, we face a challenge of economic diversification as we approach the end of the life of the Henderson Mine, which provides a large portion of our property tax base. There are hundreds of mine claims that exist in undeveloped or under-developed areas, many of which are very near headwater streams. The rule will help us balance the need for diversification while providing the necessary protection for streams and wetlands as we encourage development of all kinds.

Finally, I will conclude by conveying that this issue extends beyond my duties as an elected official, or even the economic benefits provided by clean water. As someone who grew up hunting and fishing with my father throughout Colorado, I have a deeply personal connection to clean water. My outdoor pursuits begin in the early summer chasing trout at elevations of 10,000 feet just above my home. By fall, I follow these same headwaters as they flow into the South Platte, and meander northeast of Denver to the agricultural communities of Brush and Fort Morgan where I hunt waterfowl. The Clean Water Act is an indispensable part of providing those hunting and fishing opportunities and passing America's sporting tradition across generations. In all my time spent on the water, I see firsthand a simple truth: what happens upstream in the headwaters and connected wetlands makes its way downstream to our rivers and streams. The proposed rule simply recognizes this reality.

From a personal passion about hunting and angling to my responsibility as a county commissioner to provide clean water for drinking and outdoor recreation, I strongly support the clean water rulemaking. The EPA and Corps of Engineers can, and undoubtedly will provide more clarity to interested parties about what waters are and are not covered. I urge the committee to allow this process to play out without delaying, derailing, or significantly altering the intent of the rule.

———

Dr. FLEMING. Thank you, Mr. Mauck.

The Chair now recognizes Mr. William Buzbee, Professor of Law, Georgetown University Law Center in Washington, DC, for 5 minutes to give your testimony.

---

[8] Local officials support the administration's proposal to protect clean water: http://org.salsalabs.com/o/2155/p/salsa/web/common/public/content?content_item_KEY=12837.

STATEMENT OF WILLIAM W. BUZBEE, PROFESSOR OF LAW, GEORGETOWN UNIVERSITY LAW CENTER, WASHINGTON, DC

Mr. BUZBEE. I also will focus on the Waters of the United States regulation, and I will make seven brief points, several of which relate to the opening remarks.

Point one is the extent of federally protected waters matters to much more than just wetlands or what some people sometimes characterize as land that should not be protected. The Clean Water Act and Waters of the United States is not just about marginal waters. The Waters of the United States jurisdiction is central to all of the Clean Water Act. So, as you think about the extent of Federal protection, you have to think not just about Section 404 dredge and fill, but you also have to think about Section 402's permitting of industrial discharges, as well as other efforts to protect water quality, protect drinking water, aquatic habitat, and buffer against storm surges and flooding.

Also, as Ranking Member Huffman mentioned, this has been—for, actually, decades—for about 30 years, was an issue of bipartisan consensus, that protecting of waters broadly—and, in fact, much more broadly through the Reagan administration—was an area of bipartisan agreement. In the *Rapanos* case itself, I represented a bipartisan group of former EPA administrators who were aligned with the Bush administration in arguing for ongoing protection of waters. There is reason for this bipartisan agreement; this is of great importance.

Point two, there have been a number—relates to this question of whether the rulemaking is legitimate. I have heard a brief reference earlier, and certainly have heard from critics, a question if there is room for rulemaking here, as though there is kind of an illegitimacy to the rulemaking exercise that the Army Corps of Engineers and EPA have proposed. Very importantly, six members of the Supreme Court in the *Rapanos* case called specifically for regulation to clear up the law. Earlier, a unanimous Supreme Court on the same issue, *Riverside Bayview Homes*, called for rulemaking to bring clarity to the law, and also point out the need for expert regulatory judgments.

There is no doubt that rulemaking is a legitimate exercise. People may disagree about what exactly is protected, but the idea that this is appropriate for rulemaking really is beyond disagreement.

Point three, people have also talked about broad overreach. And certainly the water grab title of today's hearing reflects a concern with Federal overreach. Very importantly, this proposed rule did not expand on Federal jurisdiction. In fact, it did several important things. Most importantly, it took a number of areas of ongoing debate and disagreement, and very explicitly, in Section 328.3(b), specified a whole slew of categories that are no longer going to be subject to Federal jurisdiction. And that is the first time there has been such explicit carve-out in these regulations.

Point four, there has long been a concern with protecting waters for no logical reason. And, in particular, the idea there is not science to back up the protections. What the Army Corps and EPA did here is they went and gathered the best peer-reviewed science on waters, and their connectivity and protections, collected that massive data, put it out for notice and comment, allowed comments, and took almost 9 months to issue the final report this past January. Then the regulations tied directly into that massive, comprehensive survey of peer-reviewed science on what is protected. This is, I think, something we should all applaud.

Point five, there is a huge reduction in Federal power in this regulation. For decades—for 30 years, roughly—there was a commerce-linked sweep-up provision in the regulations about the Clean Water Act. If there was a commerce and industrial link, the Federal Government had power to protect waters, even if there might have been other questions about whether they deserved protection. That has been deleted explicitly, and substituted instead for science-based protection.

Point six, there have been a number—has to do with this risk that kind of everything will lead to illegality and liability under the law. Very importantly, you can only be liable under the statute if you have a jurisdictional water, and you have a discharge into that water. And many of the sorts of conduct people have pointed to simply do not involve a discharge, and hence, could never give rise to liability.

Last point, this has been a lengthy and contentious rulemaking process. Public statements indicate EPA and the Corps have heard criticisms. They have explicitly indicated a plan to cut back in some areas where there have been particularly vociferous criticisms. And I hope that this committee and Congress will allow this rulemaking process to come to its conclusion. Thank you.

[The prepared statement of Mr. Buzbee follows:]

PREPARED STATEMENT OF WILLIAM W. BUZBEE, PROFESSOR OF LAW, GEORGETOWN UNIVERSITY LAW CENTER, WASHINGTON, DC

My name is William Buzbee. I am a Professor of Law at Georgetown University Law Center. I am also a member-scholar of the not-for-profit regulatory policy think-tank the Center for Progressive Reform.

I am pleased to accept this committee's invitation to testify regarding "Proposed Federal Water Grabs and Their Potential Impacts on States, Water Users, and Landowners." I will focus in my testimony on the new proposed "Waters of the United States" regulations published in the Federal Register by the Army Corps of Engineers (the Army Corps) and the U.S. Environmental Protection Agency (EPA) on April 21, 2014. As a professor asked to testify due to my expertise, not as a partisan or representative of any organization, I will seek to provide context leading to these proposed regulations, comment on the choices made by EPA and the Army Corps, and assess the legality and logic of the proposed regulations. Because these regulations are now nearing the end of a lengthy notice and comment process, undergoing review now by the Office of Management and Budget's Office of Information and Regulatory Affairs, I will also briefly comment on why, at this point, allowing EPA and the Army Corps to finish this participatory and judicially scrutinized process makes sense.

My background and past involvement with the "Waters of the United States" question:

This is not my first involvement with the question of what is protected as a "Water of the United States" under the CWA. I have been involved in past related Supreme Court litigation and legislative hearings.

As a result of my work on environmental law and federalism, I served as co-counsel for an unusual bipartisan amicus brief filed in *United States* v. *Rapanos*, 547 U.S. 715 (2006) (*Rapanos*). This brief was filed on behalf of a bipartisan group of four former Administrators of the U.S. Environmental Protection Agency (EPA). Those former U.S. EPA Administrators had served under Presidents Nixon, Ford, Carter, the first President Bush, and President Clinton. Despite their different party backgrounds and years of service, all four agreed on the importance of retaining longstanding regulations protecting America's waters. This bipartisan EPA Administrators' brief was also aligned in *Rapanos* with the George W. Bush administration's arguments before the Supreme Court, several dozen states, many local governments, and an array of environmental groups as well as hunting and fishing interests.

This substantial, bipartisan coalition, including the Bush administration, all asked the Supreme Court to uphold longstanding regulatory and statutory interpretations regarding what is protected as a ''Water of the United States,'' emphasizing the centrality of the ''waters'' determination to all of the Clean Water Act. After all, although this question of what are protected ''waters'' is often discussed with a focus on wetlands and tributaries and especially dredging and filling restrictions long set by Section 404 of the Clean Water Act, the ''waters'' issue is the key jurisdictional hook for virtually all of the Clean Water Act. This includes, among other things, direct pollution industrial discharges under Section 402 of the Clean Water Act and its National Pollutant Discharge Elimination System (NPDES) program, as well as oil spill and water quality components of the Act.

Since the Court's splintered and confusing ruling in *Rapanos*, I testified in House and Senate hearings on implications, potential fixes, and regulatory responses in 2006, 2007, 2008, and 2014. I have continued to follow developments on this proposed rule and body of law.

Earlier in my legal career, I counseled industry, municipalities and governmental authorities, states and environmental groups about environmental law, pollution control, and land use issues under all of the major Federal environmental laws, as well as state and local laws. As a scholar, I have written extensively about related issues, with a special focus in recent years on regulatory federalism, especially environmental laws and their frequent reliance on overlapping Federal, state and local environmental roles. I have published books with Cornell and Cambridge University Presses, and Wolters Kluwer/Aspen. My publications have appeared in *Stanford Law Review, Cornell Law Review, NYU Law Review, Michigan Law Review, University of Pennsylvania Law Review, Harvard Environmental Law Review,* and in an array of other journals and books. In addition to teaching at Georgetown, I previously taught at Emory University and have been a visiting professor at Columbia, Cornell, Georgetown and Illinois Law Schools.

My testimony, in brief:

These proposed regulations and a massive accompanying science report referenced and summarized in the Federal Register notice—and that science report has now been finalized—are an attempt to reduce uncertainties created by three Supreme Court decisions bearing on what sorts of ''waters'' can be federally protected under the Clean Water Act. Furthermore, the proposed rule and science report are directly responsive to the pleas and rulings of a majority of U.S. Supreme Court justices.

I will make seven main points in this testimony:

First, I will explain very briefly how the question of what ''waters'' are protected matters not just for wetlands and tributary protections, but for industrial discharges of pollution. Furthermore, the various types of waters protected perform many functions of importance to businesses and governments at all levels. Business, health, recreational, and environmental interests are all at stake here. Surely this committee will hear from some business interests arguing against the proposal of the Army Corps and EPA, but business interests are undoubtedly on both sides of this issue, with hunting, fishing, boating, recreation, and tourism linked businesses especially dependent on protection of America's waters. And because pollution and filling of America's waters threaten low cost but high value wetlands functions and waters used for agricultural purposes and for drinking water, and also water quality in drought prone areas, the despoiling or filling of America's waters would be immensely costly. In addition, state and local governments are also on both sides of this issue. Degraded water quality can lead to costly obligations for state and local governments. Of great importance, legislators and other critics make both a scientific and legal error when they assume that periodically dry areas cannot be worth protecting as a water of the United States. No majority of the Supreme Court has ever so held, and the science contradicts this view. After all, much of the United States is often dry if not suffering from drought; when waters do flow, those channeling and connecting geographic features are of critical importance and require protection against pollutant discharges that will degrade precious and scarce water.

Second, I will show how the regulatory choices reflected in these regulations are responsive to Supreme Court law and also the views of a majority of the Supreme Court that regulations on this issue are needed and appropriate.

Third, these proposed regulations reveal that EPA and Army Corps have responded to criticisms of supposed limitless claims of Federal power by retaining and solidifying exemptions.

Fourth, the regulations link a massive survey of peer-reviewed science of waters' functions with a tiered and nuanced approach. This approach answers criticism that the Federal Government is going too far and protecting areas of no value relevant to the Clean Water Act. If critics have found flaws in the science or proposed regulatory categories, they surely have participated in this notice and comment process and called for adjustments in the final rule.

Fifth, in the initial heated attacks on these proposed regulations, critics failed to note and credit a major change that removes the most expansive and least water-linked historic grounds for Federal claims of jurisdiction. The proposed regulation deleted power to regulate "other waters" based on showing that the harming activity or uses of the waters were linked to industry or commerce. This was, in effect, a commerce-linked sweep up provision. Instead, the proposed rule links Clean Water Act jurisdiction to what the best peer-reviewed science indicates deserves protection. This science-based effort should be applauded, even in a time of partisan acrimony.

Sixth, past hearings and public comments about this rule at times reveal a fundamental confusion. For liability and permit obligations to arise under CWA in connection with farming and other typical land and water uses, a discharge of pollutants must be involved. Basically, neither ordinary farming activities nor basic uses of lands, wetlands, and other covered waters are prohibited. It is the act of discharging pollutants subject to Section 402 or Section 404 permits that typically creates permitting obligations. (Oil spill prevention obligations are subject to their own separate measures that are not relevant here.) Hence, many activities are non-events under the CWA, and most actions that are covered are subject to permits that typically constrain but allow activities. If someone discharges pollutants into or destroys a protected water without a required permit or in violation of a permit, then liability arises.

Seventh, and last, I will discuss the implications of where this proposed rule stands in the regulatory process. Because it is near final, EPA, the Army Corps, and many thousands of people and organizations have expended vast resources on this rule. We all should wait and see how EPA and the Corps have addressed the many comments and concerns, whether supportive or critical.

Point I: The extent of federally protected waters matters to far more than just wetlands regulation and explains the longstanding Federal bipartisan consensus

The question of what "waters" are federally protected is not a matter that only concerns allegedly marginal waters that, as often presented by critics of the longstanding protective consensus, look more like land or involve the outermost reaches of wetlands protection. The question of what are protected "Waters of the United States" concerns the very linchpin of Federal Clean Water Act jurisdiction. It does indeed supply the hook for Section 404 "dredge and fill" coverage, but also provides the jurisdictional prerequisite for Section 402's requirement of permits for industrial pollution discharges under the National Pollution Discharge Elimination System (or NPDES). It also underpins efforts to protect water quality, protect drinking water, provide habitat, and buffer against storm surges and flooding. Furthermore, since the 1970s and still today on the Supreme Court, the longstanding consensus has been to protect far more than just waters used in the literal sense for shipping-linked navigation.

It is critical to remember that the Clean Water Act has been one of America's great success stories, helping to restore many of America's rivers from highly polluted conditions to water that often now is clean enough for fishing, recreation, and even drinking water. The Act also greatly reduced the pre-Clean Water Act tendency to see wetlands as worthless and appropriate for filling. Many of the countries we compete with for talent and business vitality suffer from a hugely degraded environment. Our cleaner environment is a major comparative advantage in the increasingly globalized economy. After-the-fact efforts to clean polluted waters are costly, and harms to health, business, governmental, and recreation interests when a water is polluted can be vast.

Despite the great progress in improving U.S. water quality, many parts of the country still suffer from degraded water quality, and threats to wetlands and tributaries still arise. Everyone shares a common interest in protecting water quality and wetlands' hugely valuable functioning. Nevertheless, individuals may see business advantage in being able to pollute with impunity or convert for private gain a tributary or wetland into land for development or other commercial use, even if others downstream are economic losers. Hence, despite a broad consensus that America's rivers, tributaries and wetlands should be protected, clashes over particular applications of the law are a near constant. All environmental protection laws, by their very nature, ask for a degree of restraint, forbearance, and attention to shared interests and resources. Congress, and under the CWA EPA and the Army Corps, play a critical role in protecting our critically important and shared water resources. That the CWA is one of America's great success stories, and a success with bipartisan roots, should not be forgotten.

Point II: The new proposed "Waters of the United States" regulations are an appropriate response to the Supreme Court's recent cases:

Protecting jurisdictional waters was an area of bipartisan consensus right through the recent Bush administration. Until the 2001 Supreme Court *Solid Waste Agency of Northern Cook County* v. *U.S. Army Corps of Engineers*, 531 U.S. 159 (2001) (*SWANCC*) decision, the law and underlying regulations reflected a stable bipartisan consensus of almost 30 years that protection of America's waters through stable Part 328 regulations was good policy. A unanimous Court deferred to agency line-drawing about what sorts of waters deserved protection in *United States* v. *Riverside Bayview Homes*, 474 U.S. 121 (1985). However, *SWANCC* and then *United States* v. *Rapanos*, 547 U.S. 715 (2006) (*Rapanos*) unsettled that longstanding bipartisan consensus, breeding legal uncertainty that the new Army Corps and EPA regulations seek to address. Greater regulatory clarity and explicit reference to the relevant best science could reduce such uncertainty, both protecting waters that matter and reducing regulatory uncertainty and costs that benefit no one.

Issuing new clarifying regulations on "waters" was explicitly embraced by a majority of Supreme Court justices in *Rapanos* and is consistent with 40 years of CWA understandings. The act of rulemaking is in no way illegitimate. A six justice majority in *Rapanos* embraced the role of expert regulation to clarify the appropriate line between land and water. This included Chief Justice Roberts, who bemoaned the lack of responsive clarifying regulations post-*SWANCC*, and Justice Kennedy, who penned a swing vote opinion that is widely viewed as the most authoritative *Rapanos* opinion. Justice Kennedy fleshed out how a "significant nexus" needs to be shown to federally protect some waters whose linkages to navigable waters and functioning makes them of possibly marginal importance; "alone or in combination," the relationship with navigable waters must be more than "speculative or insubstantial." *Rapanos*, 547 U.S. at 780. Justice Kennedy explicitly recognized that many questions about what sorts of waters deserve protection could be addressed via categories set forth by regulation. The four dissenters, all of whom joined an opinion by Justice Stevens, would have affirmed the regulators' judgments attacked in *Rapanos*; they emphasized the importance of judicial deference to expert regulatory judgments about what waters should be protected.

Thus, six justices embraced an ongoing role for regulation to bring clarity to the law. In addition, an earlier unanimous Supreme Court in *Riverside Bayview Homes* embraced deference to regulatory judgments about where to draw the line between land and water. There undoubtedly remains legitimate room for regulations to bring greater clarity to this body of law.

The proposed regulations at issue in today's hearing respond directly and reasonably to these Supreme Court calls. They protect some waters by category, basing that judgment on a comprehensive review of peer-reviewed science about the linkages, value and functions of such categories of waters. Some other types of waters are identified as possibly falling under Federal jurisdiction, but the jurisdictional determination has to follow a water site-specific review to see if a "significant nexus" exists adequate to justify Federal protection. Furthermore, the proposed regulations offer additional guidance about what "significant nexus" analysis should consider, building on Justice Kennedy's *Rapanos* language and providing additional guidance for what regulators and those seeking a jurisdictional determination should consider.

Hence, by protecting some waters by category and others on a case-by-case basis if satisfying "significant nexus" analysis, and in all instances linking such regulatory judgments to a comprehensive survey of peer-reviewed science, the Army Corps and EPA have respected Supreme Court edicts and signals. Furthermore, these proposed regulations also show fealty to the Clean Water Act's explicit textually stated goal of protecting the "chemical, physical, and biological integrity" of America's waters by reducing pollution discharges and requiring permits before discharging any pollutants into such waters, whether in the form of industrial pollution or fill.

I am aware that the proposed regulations have been much criticized by some for how they deal with some categories of tributaries and ditches, with claims that they go too far in light of common agricultural practices or common road or railroad features, for example. EPA and the Corps have had to review such comments and have surely also consulted with other relevant departments and agencies. Comments from EPA indicate that responsive changes on some of these issues are likely. If, as critics claim, EPA and the Corps ignore science or salient and accurate comments and criticisms, the final rule will be legally vulnerable and will either be challenged in court or possibly subject to petitions for regulatory correction. But maybe those comments are overblown, or have been heard and led to regulatory improvements. We should know soon.

Point III: The proposed regulations make explicit several categories of activities or waters not subject to Federal jurisdiction

A persistent refrain in recent years and regarding the proposed regulations under discussion today is that the jurisdiction being claimed borders on the limitless. Today's hearing, with its "Federal water grabs" title, evidently reflects similar concerns. Federal jurisdiction under this law has long been expansive, but the proposed rule did not, in fact, expand on Federal jurisdiction. This claim of limitless Federal power is most evidently erroneous in light of the proposal's creation of both categorically protected waters and others that must be assessed on a case-by-case basis.

However, the proposed regulations go further, in new Section 328.3(b) making explicit that several types of otherwise potentially debatable waters are not "Waters of the United States." These include (with additional more precise language): waste treatment systems; prior converted cropland; several sorts of ditches that are upland or do not contribute flow to otherwise regulated waters; and several types of "features" such as artificially irrigated areas that would revert to upland without irrigation water, artificial lakes, ponds, pools and ornamental waters, construction-linked water-filled depressions, groundwater, and gullies, rills and non-wetland swales. Several of these exemptions appear to be in direct answer to criticisms in court briefs and congressional testimony that Federal jurisdiction has bordered on the limitless.

Point IV: The proposed regulations' link to a massive survey of peer-reviewed science about waters' connectivity, values and function responds to the most prevalent criticism of "waters" Federal jurisdiction and puts all on notice

Over the past decade, a common claim of critics of Federal jurisdiction has been that waters—or sometimes lands—can and are claimed to be protected for no reason relevant to the Clean Water Act's purposes. And on this issue and in other battles over regulation, critics in Congress, the courts, and in the academy have called for "sound science" and "peer-reviewed" science to underpin regulatory judgments. The Army Corps and EPA have taken this to heart, for the first time pulling together a massive survey of peer-reviewed publications about the connectivity, values, and functions of various types of waters. This report was last year released in draft form, reviewed by the Science Advisory Board, and was made public for review and comment. On January 15, 2015, EPA announced in the Federal Register release of a final version of this report. In addition, the Corps and EPA in their proposed regulation's Federal Register notice explained how they interpreted this report and the science in deciding what types of waters are categorically protected, subject case-by-case to "significant nexus" analysis, or not protected.

This sort of notice and comment process and public vetting of the accompanying science report, with the overt linkages to the proposed "Waters of the United States" rule, have provided a valuable open, transparent, and judicially challengeable process. Supporters and critics have now had an opportunity to critique this report. We will soon be able to assess if the final rule is fairly based on the overwhelming peer-reviewed science that confirms the functional importance of many types of waters.

Point V: The Army Corps and EPA in the proposed regulations deleted the long-standing "other waters" commerce-linked sweep-up provision, instead linking protections to science and limiting Federal power

In the proposed regulations, a longstanding additional grounds for Federal jurisdiction has been deleted. This provision, the former Section 328.3(a)(3) "other waters" paragraphs, provided Federal jurisdiction to protect over a dozen sorts of waters upon a showing that their "use, degradation or destruction . . . could affect interstate or foreign commerce" or be used by "interstate or foreign travelers" for "recreational or other purposes," for fishing-linked commerce, or for "industrial purposes by industries in interstate commerce." This provision basically identified types of waters but made them protectable based on their commerce-linked uses or values. This regulation was consistent with longstanding understandings of the 1972 Clean Water Act amendments and the congressionally intended reach of Federal power. However, both the *SWANCC* and *Rapanos* decisions raised questions about whether Clean Water Act jurisdiction could focus on a water's commercial or industrial uses or the impacts of a water's degradation without regard to the water's functions or links to navigable waters.

I will not here opine on whether this section's deletion was legally necessary or prudent. I will, however, note that the Corps and EPA answered critics and eliminated uncertainty by deleting this section in favor of linking *all* jurisdictional "Waters of the United States" determinations to what the science shows, as applied to the particular sites and activities at issue. Since most pollution and filling activity is undoubtedly commercial and industrial in nature, and little today is not linked to interstate commerce, this regulatory deletion is a significant concession and reduction in Federal power. Again, the proposed regulations link regulation to peer-reviewed science and cut back on the broadest possible grounds for jurisdiction.

Point VI: An Unpermitted Discharge of a Pollutant is a Central Prerequisite for CWA Liability, Not Ordinary Uses of Lands and Waters

Both in past legislative hearings and in many statements about this proposed rule, critics have asserted that virtually everything farmers and others do in lands near waters and around or in supposed waters will now create indeterminate liability or legal prohibitions. These claims seem to be rooted in a misunderstanding of the CWA. Apart from some provisions applicable to oil spill planning that require preventive planning, permitting obligations and linked liabilities under the CWA only arise when a person will be discharging pollutants from a point source into a jurisdictional water. Section 402 industrial discharges and Section 404 "dredge and fill" permits are most relevant here. Most ordinary agricultural activities and other uses of lands and waters simply do not constitute covered discharges. First, as mentioned above, there are explicit statutory as well as regulatory carveouts, especially for categories of agricultural activity. In addition, assorted "nationwide" or "general" permits create presumptive permission for some categories of activities. And not everything is a point source; many sorts of pollutant flows, especially connected to agriculture or flowing across lands or roads, are nonpoint sources and not reached by the CWA. It is when someone decides to dump pollutants or destroy a water, yet without a permit, that legal liability arises. (Again, oil spill prevention is subject to different additional obligations.) But often such discharges will be subject to permitting and hence escape liability. So it is the unpermitted discharge of pollutants from a point source into a jurisdictional water that gives rise to concerns. Furthermore, it is extraordinarily rare that unintentional or even clearly illegal intended conduct gives rise to liability; citizens seeking to enforce the law have to give notice so there is an opportunity for cure, and government enforcers also typically try to head off trouble by telling potential law violators of their concerns. Basically, liability does not come out of the blue, but requires several stages of intentional conduct and often something approaching willful disregard of the law.

Point VII: The Notice and Comment Process Should Run Its Course So All Can Assess the Actual Final Regulation

A high stakes regulatory action like the "Waters of the United States" rule triggers vast investments of time and resources by private and public actors. Congress should let this process come to a regulatory conclusion.

EPA and the Corps have participated in hundreds of public sessions around the country about this proposal. Many thousands of hours have been spent on this rule by a vast array of interested actors, including months of surely painstaking review by EPA and the Army Corps, and now by OIRA, which tends to look at proposed rules with an eye to efficiency goals, through cost-benefit analysis, and in coordinating among sometimes clashing parts of the executive branch. During such a notice and comment process, the executive branch has to comport itself with a vast body of administrative law that the courts police; agencies need to read comments, respond to salient criticisms, and justify the final regulatory choices in light of statutory language, court decisions, and relevant science and facts. If an agency violates any of these obligations, courts can and do step in and reject the agency's action. Or, sometimes, a flaw that is found and pointed out by critics will lead an agency to make further revisions, sometimes with yet another more focused notice and comment process. All of us—whether in or outside government—must be stewards of limited private and taxpayer resources. To try to block a new rule without seeing what it actually looks like in its final form is both unnecessary and threatens just such waste. If the final rule is deeply flawed in its final form, then corrective actions can be sought in Congress, with the agencies again, or in the courts. And if it is a sound and responsive document, then much of the criticism may abate. America will benefit if important waters are again protected, and all will benefit from less regulatory uncertainty. At a minimum, the array of supportive and opposed constituencies will likely change when the final rule's choices are disclosed. I hope that Congress will let this regulation run its course.

Conclusion

The legal uncertainty of recent years about what are protected Federal waters has benefited no one. For those concerned about protection of America's waters, regulatory uncertainty has led to regulatory forbearance, problematic or erroneous regulatory and judicial decisions, and increased regulatory costs. By now linking the "Waters of the United States" question to peer-reviewed science and clarifying which waters are subject to categorical or case-by-case protection and revealing the reasons for such judgments, the Corps and EPA have moved the law in the direction of certainty and clarity. This is an area calling for difficult, expert regulatory judgments. There was a reason for the 30 years of bipartisan consensus in favor of broadly protecting America's waters. These proposed regulations, if finalized in a substantially similar form but with explanations and changes addressing concerns voiced during the process, could once again bring clarity and stability to the law, while also respecting the protective mandates of the Clean Water Act. We are nearing the end of lengthy, intensive, and contentious regulatory process. I hope that Congress will allow the process to reach its conclusion so we can all assess the legality and wisdom of the newly released final rule. Little is bipartisan these days, but protection of America's waters is surely valued on both sides of the aisle and embraced broadly at the Federal, state, and local level. Certainly no one can be against the protection of America's invaluable water resources. Let's see if the final rule will deserve broad support.

————

Dr. FLEMING. Thank you, Mr. Buzbee. I would now like to recognize Congressman Newhouse to introduce our next witness on this panel.

Mr. NEWHOUSE. Thank you, Mr. Chairman. I am delighted to be able to introduce and welcome Mr. Tom Myrum. He is one of the most respected and recognized voices in Washington State's water community.

For the last 20 years, Tom has been serving as Executive Director and Counsel of the Washington State Water Resources Association, which is the coordinating agency for irrigation districts in the state of Washington. Tom is also the immediate past president of the National Water Resources Association, which represents water users throughout the western and southeastern United States.

I should say Tom grew up in Wyoming, graduated the University of Utah, received his JD from the University of Idaho College of Law. A member of both Washington and Oregon Bar Associations, he has worked with irrigation districts in Oregon before taking his current role with the WSWRA.

And Tom, I certainly welcome you. I know you understand the challenges of Western water law, and look forward to your contribution to this conversation. Thank you.

Thank you, Mr. Chairman.

Dr. FLEMING. Therefore, Mr. Myrum, you are now recognized for 5 minutes.

STATEMENT OF TOM MYRUM, EXECUTIVE DIRECTOR, WASHINGTON STATE WATER RESOURCES ASSOCIATION, OLYMPIA, WASHINGTON

Mr. MYRUM. Thank you. Chairman Fleming, Ranking Member Huffman, thank you for this invitation to speak before you today. I won't read from the script, because my eyes are getting worse every day, and it seems like today was one of the worst. But I will say that irrigation districts westwide are into about 150 years of development, either privately or with the assistance of the Bureau of Reclamation through the Reclamation Act of 1902. As a result, we have been able to reclaim much of the West and cause it to bloom, turn it into fertile agricultural land, which has really built a very strong agricultural economic base in the West.

We are no strangers to the Clean Water Act. It has been mentioned earlier that ditches are exempt from the Clean Water Act. If only that were so, if someone could put that in writing, we would breathe much easier. And I can give you some specific examples.

In Washington State—I will speak specifically, since it is most close to my knowledge—Clean Water Act has visited us in a few different ways. In our irrigation delivery canals and drains, some of them are already on the 303(d) list of water quality limited stream segments. They have new space standards applied to them, and efforts to try to remove them through use attainability analyses have often been, well, difficult, if not impossible. The EPA and the State Department of Ecology find that process very cumbersome, and we would like that we can move that. But the point I want to make is it is both delivery canals and return flow drains where that applies.

We are currently subject to 402 permits, NPDES permits, for the use of aquatic pesticides to remove the aquatic weeds from the canals. As a result, when we put the pesticides both into delivery canals and drains, we must use these permits.

In 2007, after a couple years of working with the Bureau of Reclamation and the Corps of Engineers, we were successful, with the help of NWRA, in getting regulatory guidance on our 0702, which lined out when irrigation district drains are not 404-jurisdictional. That was very helpful. And, as a matter of fact, it was one of our state fisheries people who had asked the Corps of Engineers to look to see if these drains were, indeed, 404-jurisdictional. A great interface with the Corps of Engineers then led to that regulatory guidance letter.

One of the interesting facts about that is, if you went to the Seattle District or the Walla Walla District, you might get a slightly different reading of that regulatory guidance letter. I bring that up for the point that, with the new clarification of this very large rule, it is entirely possible that this specific regulatory guidance letter, and many more, could be reinterpreted. They could be rewritten, thus leading to the jurisdictional elements of our drains suddenly having to have 404 permits: something we haven't had to have to date.

Let me give an example of some positives in the Clean Water Act. The TMDL, appropriately set in the Lower Yakima River, where Congressman Newhouse's district, the Sunnyside Valley Irrigation District, gets their water—two drains were listed for TMDLs on sediments. The districts, the Rosa District and the Sunnyside District, both worked together with their farmers to meet the goal of the TMDL in less than the 10 years allowed. They did it within, I think, about a 3-year period. And, as a result, they got two environmental excellence awards from our then-Governor Locke. So, the irrigation districts have familiarity with the Clean Water Act, and being positive actors within it, and getting to good environmental results.

What we see here from this very large clarification is it will lend itself toward reinterpretation by the agencies and, ultimately, find its way back through the courts to determine whether or not the clarification was, indeed, an appropriate clarification. And so, the cycle works its way back through, and the court, from *Rapanos*, will ultimately get to decide if what the agency did was correct. This could be, then, a never-ending cycle, leading to a lot of concern within the regulated community as to what the standard truly is.

And I thank you very much for this opportunity to testify.

[The prepared statement of Mr. Myrum follows:]

PREPARED STATEMENT OF TOM MYRUM, WASHINGTON STATE WATER RESOURCES ASSOCIATION, ON BEHALF OF NATIONAL WATER RESOURCES ASSOCIATION

Chairman Fleming, Ranking Member Huffman, and members of the subcommittee, thank you for giving me the opportunity to appear before you today, and for your attention to the many water challenges facing our Nation. My name is Tom Myrum, I am the Executive Director of the Washington State Water Resources Association. I am also the immediate past President of the National Water Resources Association, more commonly known as NWRA. I am here today to testify on behalf of NWRA and its members from around the United States.

NWRA is a nonpartisan, nonprofit federation made up of agricultural and municipal water providers, state associations, and individuals dedicated to the conservation, enhancement and efficient management of our Nation's most important natural resource, water. The NWRA represents a diverse group of agricultural and municipal water users and water providers from throughout the American West and portions of the southern United States. Our members provide clean water to millions of individuals, families, agricultural producers and other businesses in a manner that supports communities, the economy and the environment.

For more than 80 years our members have worked, oftentimes in partnership with Federal agencies, to provide water in a manner that provides both economic and ecosystem benefits to communities. NWRA is committed to working with the Congress and the agencies to provide a clearly defined, efficient process for all permitting requirements.

Our members' ability to provide the water that our Nation depends on is directly influenced by the role and scope of Federal regulation.

IMPORTANCE OF WATER

I'm here today because water is a fundamental element for life and our economy, but until it is gone many Americans pay little attention to it. Federal regulations have a direct affect on NWRA and our members' ability to deliver this vital resource. We are blessed to have one of the most comprehensive water infrastructure systems the world has ever seen, and while not perfect, this infrastructure allows almost all Americans to access water with the turn of a tap. It is truly a wonder of the modern world.

The development of this system was not always easy and sometimes was met with failure. In fact some of the West's most iconic figures including "Buffalo Bill" Cody and Sheriff Pat Garrett tried and failed to develop water systems. Despite these challenges our forbearers in water persisted because they saw the vital need for access to water. This is true not only in the United States, but also worldwide.

Water is one of the cornerstones of our society and a building block for life. Another building block is food. According to the USDA, the United States is responsible for approximately 20 percent of the world's food exports by volume. Input costs for U.S. agricultural production affect costs both domestically and globally. Keeping food affordable is extremely important because price spikes can have disproportionate adverse affects on vulnerable populations. According to U.N. and World Bank figures, price spikes in 2008 drove 110 million people into poverty and added 44 million to the undernourished globally. As the world's population continues to grow in coming decades, the need to produce food will also grow. It is estimated that by 2050 the demand for food will grow by 70 percent.

Food production in the United States must play a role in meeting this demand. This is a daunting challenge but one that NWRA members are ready to help our Nation's agricultural producers meet. Our Nation's farmers and ranchers have successfully doubled U.S. food production over the last half century. Much of this improvement has come during a time when agriculture is working to become more efficient in its water use. According to the USGS, since peaking in 1980 water used for irrigation has dropped from almost 150 billion gallons per day to about 115 billion gallons a day in 2010. Since 2005 alone, 950 thousand more acres of land have been put into irrigated agricultural production while water use has been reduced 9 percent.

Increased production with less water is made possible because agricultural water users are making significant investments in water use technologies. As an example, NWRA members in New Mexico have invested in subsurface drip irrigation systems that help reduce water lost to evaporation. Producers in Arizona are laser leveling their fields to help reduce water lost to runoff. In my home state of Washington irrigators are using SCADA technology to help measure and respond to water demands in real time, which yields water savings.

Despite improvements in agricultural water use the world remains a thirsty place. According to the USGS the average American uses between 80 and 100 gallons of water a day. Much of this water is used for sanitary needs. This 80- to 100-gallon figure is only part of the picture of water use in the United States.

Last week, the *Los Angles Times* had a number of articles discussing the water footprint for a variety of crops. It also featured an interactive page on it's Web site which allows you to construct a meal and get the total water footprint associated with that meal. This web page featured a "random plate" option that builds a meal for you, selecting a protein, grain, vegetable and beverage for you and totaling the associated water use. The random plate I selected, which is pictured below, gave me a meal consisting of:

- 8 ounces of chickpeas with an associated water footprint of 608.6 gallons;
- 6 ounces of wheat bread with an associated water footprint of 86.8 gallons;
- 8 ounces of carrots with an associated water footprint of 7.4 gallons; and
- 8 ounces of wine with an associated water footprint of 27.8 gallons

This heart health meal had a total water value of 730 gallons.

Figure 1: LA Times Food Water Footprint [1]

Food isn't the only product with a water footprint. As an example, a cotton T-shirt can utilize approximately 700 gallons of water, a 32-megabyte computer chip—which weighs about 2 grams—has a water footprint of about 8 gallons, and a single

---

[1] http://graphics.latimes.com/food-water-footprint/.

piece of paper has a water footprint of around 2.6 gallons. This means that one copy of my testimony has a water footprint of 26 gallons.

It is important to note that a water footprint is only one part of a complex picture. A product's water footprint is only one indicator that doesn't actually represent the water contained in a product. It considers larger issues associated with the full supply chain. Water is still an important component of input and should be considered but it isn't the only component that should be considered.

Should we stop growing avocados in California and instead only purchase them from more water rich places like New Zeeland? If so what about other environmental factors like the carbon footprint needed to transport that avocado nearly 9,000 miles to grocery store shelves here in DC?

Should Intel stop building computer components in Arizona at a factory that President Obama said is an example of: "An America that attracts the next generation of good manufacturing jobs. An America where we build stuff and make stuff and sell stuff all over the world."[2]

Should the Federal Government stop issuing final rules because, according to the Congressional Research Service, the government published 26,417 pages worth of final rules in the Federal Register in 2013?[3] That's more than 68,000 gallons of water to print just one copy of rules finalized 2013.

I ask these questions not to make light of the importance of considering water inputs, but rather to highlight the fact that these are complex questions. We use water every day in ways that most individuals don't realize. This makes addressing current and future water supply needs a major responsibility. Meeting these needs will require collaboration, creativity and flexibility. NWRA members are ready to work with the subcommittee and Federal agencies to meet these needs.

PENDING REGULATORY PROPOSALS—POTENTIAL IMPLICATIONS FOR WATER SUPPLY

NWRA and our members do not oppose regulation outright. We see value in regulations when appropriately applied and are active members of the regulated community. Our members take great pride in providing water while meeting ecosystem needs. NWRA members fully understand and support the need for keeping our waters safe and clean, not only for purposes of crop production, but also for drinking water, fish and wildlife habitat, and recreational uses. To further those goals, NWRA members continue to make necessary improvements to their systems to increase efficiencies, conservation, and environmental protections.

However, we also believe that Federal regulations are not, by default, universally good ideas. In many cases there is a fine line between appropriate regulation and unnecessary overreach. In these instances it is our responsibility to work to address these problems. That responsibility is why I am here today.

In my testimony this morning I will focus on three items: the Environmental Protection Agency (EPA) and Army Corps of Engineers (Corps) proposed rule regarding the definition of the "Waters of the United States" and its impacts on Bureau of Reclamation customers; the Forest Service's Ski Area Water Rights Clause; and the Forest Service's proposed groundwater management directive.

However, I would do the subcommittee and water users a disservice if I failed to mention that these three items are only a small sample of the numerous pending rules, regulations, or policies proposed by Federal agencies that could significantly and adversely affect water users. Last year NWRA filed 11 sets of comments on regulatory proposals. In the first quarter of this year we have filed comments on three additional items. All 14 of our comment letters highlight that Federal regulations can unnecessarily hinder water supply operations if not correctly implemented.

We file these comments because it is vital that Federal agencies understand and appreciate the complex process and unique circumstances surrounding water delivery. If our members can't do our job many of your constituents can't get water.

It is also important to note that the absence of Federal regulation does not translate to a total lack of regulation. All states have, at some level, statutes that protect water and address water quality issues. In fact some of these protections are more stringent than Federal requirements and exceed the protections offered under the Federal Clean Water Act. In addition, many municipalities and water districts undertake additional efforts to protect water quality, often at great cost, without any requirement to do so.

---

[2] https://www.whitehouse.gov/the-press-office/2012/01/25/remarks-president-intel-ocotillo-campus-chandler-az.

[3] https://fas.org/sgp/crs/misc/R43056.pdf.

CLEAN WATER ACT AND PROPOSED DEFINITION OF WATERS OF THE UNITED STATES

Last year NWRA members testified before both the House Transportation and Infrastructure Committee and the House Natural Resources Committee on the pending rule defining "Waters of the United States". During these hearings it became evident that there is bipartisan interest in ensuring the Clean Water Act is appropriately applied. It also became evident that the proposed rule created an immense amount of confusion and needed clarification.

Prior to the issuance of this rule many NWRA members sought clarification to the jurisdictional questions under the Clean Water Act. Many hoped that the proposed rule would provide additional clarity that would help agencies and water users more effectively implement the Act.

The primary goal of any rulemaking should be to clarify the scope of the Federal agencies' jurisdiction under the Act. Unfortunately, the rule that has been proposed by the agencies only adds to the confusion over jurisdictional determinations. And now, almost a year after we first discussed this issue with Congress, we find ourselves back testifying again. In the intervening year the clarity we have long sought remains illusive.

Under the agencies' proposed rule all ditches are jurisdictional unless specifically exempted. The only ditches that are exempted are those which are excavated wholly in uplands, drain only uplands and have less than perennial flow or ditches that do not contribute flow to a traditional navigable water, interstate water, the territorial seas or impoundments thereof.

Contrary to EPA public statements, these exemptions are of limited utility. As an example, in many western states, ditches are often used to move water to fields for irrigation purposes or to municipal intakes. Hence, they commence at a ditch headgate "on the stream," i.e., not in an "upland". In addition, they oftentimes eventually provide return flows back to the stream after use in accordance with water court decree requirements. Further, under the proposal, the ditches themselves would be treated as jurisdictional waters even though point source discharges into the ditch that may reach a traditional navigable water will be regulated under state law.

The use of ditches is critical in meeting Western municipal and agricultural water supply needs. Most ditches are not excavated wholly in uplands or drain to another waterbody and therefore are not exempt under the current proposal.

We do not believe that Congress or the Courts ever intended for features like irrigation ditches to be jurisdictional under the Clean Water Act. The words chosen by Congress and the intent of the Act are clear: irrigation canals, ditches, and drains were not meant to be regulated under the Clean Water Act. This was reflected in the 1975 and 1977 regulations, which provided that "manmade nontidal drainage and irrigation ditches excavated on dry land are not considered waters of the United States." 40 Fed. Reg. 31, 321 (1975); 33 CFR 323.2(a)(5)(1982).

The Federal Government has a vested interest in seeing that irrigation facilities are operated and maintained in a manner that protects the public from deterioration and failure of these facilities. Without the ability to conduct necessary maintenance activities, free from time consuming and costly Federal processes, agricultural water delivery, and many of the efforts aimed at improving efficiencies, protecting public safety and conserving water, would be severely challenged, if allowed at all.

It also needs to be noted that many of the facilities that could now be jurisdictional for the first time provide flood control or public safety functions. In such cases, regular maintenance activities to maintain channel capacity are necessary to protect life and property. In addition catastrophic forest fires and floods are growing more commonplace events in the West. When these catastrophic fires occur it is essential to quickly undertake remedial activities after such events, including sediment and debris detention, in order to protect health, safety, infrastructure/property and environmental values. Categorizing all small drainages as jurisdictional, with accompanying regulatory requirements, will impede the ability to appropriately respond to such disasters and could jeopardize public safety and property.

The proposed WOTUS rule in its current form will make meeting future water and food supply needs more difficult. We hope that the final rule proposed by the agencies reflects NWRA's concerns and focuses on limiting the regulatory uncertainty of "Waters of the U.S." and jurisdiction, and not create unnecessary burdens on entities such as irrigation districts and water suppliers, whose purpose and facilities have no relationship to the originally envisioned scope of the Clean Water Act.

FOREST SERVICE SKI AREA WATER RIGHTS CLAUSE

Over the last several years the Forest Service has issued proposals relating to the management of water rights associated with ski areas and special use permits. The

Proposed Ski Area Water Rights Directive (Water Rights Directive) ostensibly appears to apply to ski areas, but we are concerned that it could have broader policy implications that would harm people, local governments and other entities that own state allocated water rights. This proposal threatens to vastly increase Forest Service control over state allocated water rights. This is counter to state law and stands to harm water users by interfering with the management and use of their state allocated water rights.

Collectively, NWRA members have spent billions of dollars investing in the development of state issued water rights and associated infrastructure in order to provide a safe and reliable water supply to their customers. Their ability to continue meeting the Nation's growing demand for clean water is dependent upon access to this vital resource. Water rights constitute a valuable property right and as such are valuable assets that are often irreplaceable.

The Water Rights Directive would require that a state allocated water right be tied to a special use permit issued by the Forest Service. Further it stipulates that these water rights can only be sold to the subsequent ski area special use permit holder and that the water can only be used in support of a ski area.

By restricting the market for a state allocated water right the Forest Service is essentially driving down the value of that water right. This amounts to a taking of property. The Forest Service seems to acknowledge this problem in the Proposed Directive and would require a water right holder to waive any claim against the United States for compensation. Specifically, the proposal states: ''The holder waives any claims against the United States for compensation for any water rights that it transfers, removes, or relinquishes as a result of the foregoing provisions; any claims for compensation in connection with imposition of restrictions on severing any water rights; and any claims for compensation in connection with imposition of any conditions on installation, operation, maintenance, and removal of water facilities in support of the ski area authorized by this permit.''

The Forest Service itself appears to admit that this provision is problematic and would adversely impact property rights and may run counter to the Fifth Amendment. In the June 23, 2014, Federal Register notice the Forest Service states that: ''The waiver provision is constitutional, because constitutional rights, including those protected by the Fifth Amendment, can be waived.'' It is disconcerting that the Forest Service, an agent of the U.S. Government, is encouraging the parties that it negotiates with to waive constitutional rights as a condition of a special use permit. Our members do not believe that waiving a constitutional right should be considered so lightly. We also have great concern that a special use permit holder should be faced with a Hobson's choice requiring the waiver of their constitutional rights in exchange for access to water.

This proposal exceeds the agency's authority as Congress has not provided the Forest Service power over water rights owned by a third party under state law. In addition, we are concerned the Proposed Directive would lead to the decreased value of a water right, would limit water management flexibility and increase the workload for both water users and the Forest Service alike.

The creation of a process through which water deliveries could be made contingent on the modification, relinquishment or surrender of a water right is unacceptable.

FOREST SERVICE GROUNDWATER PROPOSAL—PRACTICAL MANAGEMENT
CONSIDERATIONS

Last year the U.S. Forest Service proposed a directive aimed at groundwater management. Its ''Proposed Directive on Groundwater Resources Management'' (Groundwater Directive) is extremely troubling to water users. As currently drafted, the Forest Service Directive unnecessarily expands the reach of the Federal Government into an area generally regulated by the states. The Groundwater Directive is also concerning because it makes numerous mentions to adjacent non-Federal lands.

While we are extremely concerned by this proposal, we do want to state that we recognize and appreciate the efforts that the Forest Service has undertaken to communicate with our members following the initial release of the Groundwater Directive. These interactions helped establish a productive dialog and we believe that they were mutually beneficial. However, we remain concerned that the Proposed Groundwater Directive is fundamentally flawed.

The Forest Service lacks the authority to implement the Groundwater Directive and does not adequately consider the importance of state water law. It also does not appreciate the differences in water law between eastern states, individual western states and the territories. The Forest Service manages 155 National Forests and 20 National Grasslands on nearly 193 million acres of land in 44 states, Puerto Rico and the Virgin Islands. The water laws and water management needs in these areas vary greatly. As an example, the water laws and needs in New York are vastly different from the water laws and needs in New Mexico. The Agency's proposal does not sufficiently address this. One of our fundamental concerns is that the Proposed Groundwater Directive creates substantial uncertainty about the management of water supplies and the interaction of the Agency with respect to state allocated water rights.

Historically, Congress and the courts have recognized limits on the Forest Service's authority relating to the management of water resources. Congress passed the McCarran Amendment in 1952. Under the McCarran Amendment the United States waived its sovereign immunity to be sued in a dispute relating to water rights and cannot object to the application of a state law under such a proceeding. The McCarran Amendment also ratified the legal framework that the Federal Government must utilize to validate its state granted water rights, treating Federal and non-Federal water right holders alike. In addition, as noted by the Supreme Court in 1978, in *U.S.* v. *New Mexico*, this authority is not boundless. It largely extends to surface water resources and, as Justice Rehnquist stated in the opinion of the Court: "Congress intended that water would be reserved only where necessary to preserve the timber or to secure favorable water flows for private and public uses *under state law* (emphasis added)."

In addition to creating an additional permitting burden we are worried that these provisions would adversely impact water supply affordability. Millions of individuals depend on NWRA's members to provide a clean, reliable and affordable supply of water. Our members are dedicated to meeting this charge. We are concerned that the Proposed Groundwater Directive would drive up water costs. There are many portions of the Proposed Groundwater Directive that we could note to discuss these concerns but we will highlight section 2562.1 and section 2563.3.

Section 2562.1 states:

> *In lieu of accessing water from NFS lands, encourage public water suppliers and other water users to employ new treatment technology to meet water supply needs when water quality in an existing water source has degraded or become polluted.*

NWRA's members are proud to be on the cutting edge of water supply technologies and many of our members are actively engaged in researching, planning and implementing these technologies. It is unclear what the Agency would do to "encourage" water suppliers to use new treatment technologies. We believe that water supply decisions should be conducted in an environmentally sensitive manner and driven by water supply demands and community needs. Responding to climate variability and the growing demand for water will require the responsible consideration of all available options. Our members are concerned that the Proposed Groundwater Directive may unnecessarily limit these options. It is also important to note that new treatment technologies can be more costly than traditional water supply options and can also be very energy intensive.

NWRA believes that Section 2563.3 could also lead to increased water costs. It states that the Forest Service will:

> *Deny proposals to construct wells on or pipelines across NFS lands which can reasonably be accommodated on non-NFS lands and which the proponent is proposing to construct on NFS lands because they afford a lower cost and less restrictive location than non-NFS lands (FSM 2703.2).*

NWRA does not understand why the Forest Service would issue a de-facto denial of a water supply project that could yield a more affordable water supply. The Groundwater Directive does not define "reasonably." This requirement is excessively ambiguous and ignores the fact that water infrastructure can be constructed in a manner that benefits both people and the environment. Evaluating all alternatives could be a very time consuming process, and could delay already planned and vital water projects. There are few other "reasonable" alternatives to developing facilities off of NFS lands in the mountains of the western United States. In some western counties the Forest Service can hold upwards of 80 percent of the land. We also fail to understand why the Forest Service is openly embracing a policy that they know will directly increase water costs for people throughout the West.

The Groundwater Directive provides for collaboration with other Federal agencies, such as experts from the USGS, state, tribal, and local agencies, and other organizations; noticeably absent is the Bureau of Reclamation, irrigation districts, and other water providers who are the largest distributors and users of water resources, many of which have existing water systems on Forest Service lands.

Our primary concerns with the Groundwater Directive are centered on its interaction with state water law. However, I also wanted to note that this proposal wouldn't be implemented in a vacuum. We are concerned that the Forest Service will attempt to tie permit approval to the modification of a state issued water right. As discussed earlier in my testimony, the Forest Service has already attempted this in regard to ski area permitting and we are concerned that the agency will attempt to apply similar policies to water users.

CONCLUSION

NWRA and our members are proud to perform a vital service by helping to supply the water that grows food that the world depends on. Regulations have a role in our society and when appropriately implement can be beneficial. However, if implemented in their current forms the pending WOTUS, Ski Area Water Rights Directive and Groundwater Directive will make it harder to meet current and future water needs for both agricultural and municipal water users. These proposals will make it harder to respond to the challenges posed by climate change, make it harder to feed the world and grow the economy.

Meeting current and future water supply needs a major challenge. Meeting these needs will require collaboration, creativity and flexibility. NWRA members are ready to work with the subcommittee and Federal agencies to meet these needs.

Thank you for the opportunity to testify today and for your attention to the critical issues facing water users.

––––––

QUESTIONS SUBMITTED FOR THE RECORD BY THE HON. DAN NEWHOUSE TO TOM MYRUM, WASHINGTON STATE WATER RESOURCES ASSOCIATION

Question 1. Testimony presented to this committee last year indicated that current proposed water storage sites in the Yakima Basin could be impacted by the Forest Service's Groundwater Directive since many of the sites are on Forest Service lands. As you know, some of the new storage planned in the Yakima Basin would be for multiple uses, including cold-water fish flows. Would the Groundwater Directive make it harder for conservation projects like this to get built?

Answer. The Yakima Basin Integrated Plan presents each action such as the cold-water fish flow objectives as a single unified set of actions each dependent on the other. Any additional regulatory overlays could affect the entire project. The Forest Service's Groundwater Directive seeking to establish a Federal reserved groundwater right would affect the water supply balance in the Yakima Basin thus effecting the most fundamental underpinnings of the Integrated Plan. Any future attempts by the U.S. Forest Service or other Federal agency to establish water rights must be part of the state's water right system managed by the Washington State Department of Ecology. Following Ecology's necessary path will insure that water rights are allocated in accordance with the well-established prior appropriation doctrine of "first in time is first in right." Any new water right would be junior to all others.

Question 2. Throughout today's testimony, we've heard time and again that there's confusion as to what some of these proposed regulations could mean at the local level. We have also heard that there was little to no communication prior to the issuance of these proposals—particularly the Forest Service's Groundwater Directive—with the states and local governmental entities. Was there a breakdown in communication between the Federal Government and the state and local governments and water and power districts impacted by the proposals? What is the practical impact of this lack of communication?

Answer. The U.S. Forest Service's lack of communication and general disregard for the state and local impact of their misguided attempt to establish a Federal reserved groundwater right led to confusion and alarm at the local level. I can only assume that the state agencies were caught off guard at the same time. The sensitive nature of the water balance associated with a prior appropriation system of water rights, such as we have in Washington State, cannot be understated. It is hard to believe that the U.S. Forest Service professionals could not have had some appreciation for the potential chaotic impact of their proposal as it relates to water rights. Water rights establish key relationships among water users in any river basin. The U.S. Forest Service's attempt to interject themselves into this system without going through the proper process threatened to upset the delicate balance of water use and water user relationships.

Question 3. You testified that the Bureau of Reclamation's facilities could be significantly impacted by the Waters of the U.S. and the Groundwater Directive. Fortunately, the Forest Service is here to answer the latter but the Bureau of Reclamation chose not to answer questions today. Mr. Myrum, is it correct to say that the Bureau of Reclamation has made investments in Washington State and could make investments in new storage at a later point? Would these investments be impacted by both proposals?

Answer. The EPA and USACE Water of the United States jurisdictional clarifying rule injects uncertainty into any project permitting system. Projects are planned with certain permitting expectations established during the project planning phase and the environmental compliance phase. If Clean Water Act jurisdictional waters are expanded to areas not previously considered jurisdictional, it is conceivable that projects such as the Yakima Basin Integrated Plan and its numerous individual projects could face new permitting or at least the uncertainty of whether or not additional permitting is necessary. This confusion can cost time and money for any project. As I have mentioned above the U.S. Forest Service's guidance could affect the fundamental water balance in any basin. The fully appropriated Yakima Basin's water rights system would be thrown into chaos without the protection of the state's water right permitting system.

––––––

Dr. FLEMING. Thank you, Mr. Myrum.

And, finally, last, but not least, Mr. Heinen, General Manager of the Jefferson Davis Electric Co-op, from my home state of Louisiana. You are recognized, sir, for 5 minutes.

STATEMENT OF MIKE HEINEN, GENERAL MANAGER, JEFFERSON DAVIS ELECTRIC COOPERATIVE, INC., JENNINGS, LOUISIANA

Mr. HEINEN. Thank you. Chairman Fleming, Ranking Member Huffman, members of the subcommittee, thank you for inviting me to testify today. My name is Mike Heinen, I serve as General Manager of Jeff Davis Electric Cooperative Headquarters in Jennings, Louisiana.

Our member-owned, member-controlled electric cooperative provides power for nearly 10,000 residential, commercial, industrial customers across five parishes in the immediate southwest corner of our state, representing more than 30,000 consumers.

To us, in southwest Louisiana, which is home to 3 million acres of coastal wetlands, wetland does not mean wasteland. Our coast is very much an active coast, with nearly one-third of our state's population living and working on or very near the Gulf of Mexico.

We are concerned that the Environmental Protection Agency's proposed Federal water grab goes too far in disturbing a delicate public-private balance by imposing additional unnecessary permitting requirements, adding great burdens and bureaucratic red tape, while further restricting our opportunity to continue economic progress, and threatening our cooperative's ability to deliver safe, affordable, reliable electric power to our members.

In my opinion, the current rules go beyond far enough.

A prime example of the manner in which overreaching Federal policies have proven problematic and wasteful for our cooperative occurred in the wake of Hurricane Rita nearly 10 years ago. The storm completely destroyed our branch office located in Cameron, Louisiana, which was established to serve the residents and commercial consumers along the coast. A track of land was then generously donated to the cooperative by one of the cooperative's long-term directors, Mr. Charles S. Hackett. He donated 5 acres of land 25 miles north of Cameron to rebuild our branch office.

The current level of Federal oversight through the Clean Water Act caused delays and expenses to the cooperative in the form of environmental surveys, flood plain surveys, permits, and inspections that amounted to thousands of dollars being spent before the first shovel of dirt was even turned.

During that process it was discovered that 1.5 of the 5 acres was declared wetlands because of the presence of a certain species of indigenous vegetation. This land was farm land, and laid idle for several years because Mr. Hackett no longer wanted to have it farmed. It was not wetlands. Because this certain vegetation was found on the property, according to Federal guidelines, nothing could be done with the land until mitigation took place.

In order to take advantage of Mr. Hackett's generosity, Jeff Davis Electric was forced to purchase 1.5 acres of wetlands from the Federal Government in an unknown location for environmental mitigation. The cost to Jeff Davis Electric Co-op and its members was $30,000. This was an unforseen expense that had to be passed on to our consumers, who ultimately bear the cost for unnecessary, burdensome Federal oversight and regulation.

This is the type of burdensome Federal regulation that we need less of, not more. An expansion of the Clean Water Act, as currently proposed in EPA's Waters of the United States rule, would complicate, not simplify our Co-op's routine operations and maintenance. Ambiguous definitions in the proposed rule will vastly expand the reach of the Clean Water Act, cause major problems for our consumers in Louisiana's coastal plains. For instance, simply performing maintenance on our power lines, poles, and other infrastructure to ensure reliability for our customers would require additional permitting, additional costs, and unreasonable delays.

It is my personal view, and the view of Jeff Davis Electric, that the stringent Federal rules and regulations currently in place, in addition to those imposed by state and local authorities, are useful and effective in protecting our wetlands, our precious resources, and our natural habitat. The stringent existing requirements already make it difficult to build infrastructure to new commercial enterprises, and adequately maintain right-of-way to ensure cost-effective service reliability for our members.

I urge the subcommittee to seriously consider the impact of Federal rules and regulations on the people of southwest Louisiana and the members of Jeff Davis Electric, many of whom have spent their lives in the area. Our region has benefited greatly from the efforts of the state and Federal Government, as well as private agencies, to protect and preserve our wetlands. For this we are grateful. However, there is a tipping point where unnecessary mandates and restrictions intended to help our people become punitive and inhibit the ability of our economy to grow and our people to prosper. Any policies adopted by the Federal Government need to be smart and effective in achieving the desired outcome without negative consequences that diminish the ability of our rural cooperative members to continue their way of life and provide for their families. Thank you.

[The prepared statement of Mr. Heinen follows:]

PREPARED STATEMENT OF MICHAEL J. HEINEN, GENERAL MANAGER, JEFFERSON DAVIS ELECTRIC COOPERATIVE, JENNINGS, LOUISIANA

INTRODUCTION

Chairman Fleming, Ranking Member Huffman, members of the subcommittee, thank you for inviting me to testify today on "Proposed Federal Water Grabs and Their Potential Impacts on States, Water and Power Users and Landowners." My name is Michael J. Heinen and I serve as General Manager of Jeff Davis Electric Cooperative headquartered in Jennings, Louisiana. Our member-owned, member-controlled electric cooperative provides power for nearly 10,000 residential, commercial and industrial consumers across five parishes in the immediate southwestern corner of our state, representing more than 30,000 consumers. I am a proud native and life-long resident of our cooperative's service territory, which is bordered by the state of Texas to the west and the Gulf of Mexico to the south, with numerous rivers and tributaries flowing from the north and three substantial bodies of brackish water in Calcasieu, Grand and White lakes.

To us in southwest Louisiana, which is home to 3 million acres of coastal wetlands, "wetland" does not mean "wasteland." Our coast is very much an active coast with nearly one-third of our state's population living and working on or very near the Gulf of Mexico. The area's proximity to the Gulf waters makes it an attractive draw for a variety of industries including oil and gas interests, fisheries, transportation, livestock, farming and much more. As a key part of the region's economic development engine, Jeff Davis Electric serves eight natural gas processors along with other commercial and industrial enterprises. Moreover, our service area is a national leader in waterfowl and alligator harvests, is home to important state and Federal wildlife refuges which cover 285,000 acres and attract 20,000 visitors a month to the coast's 26 miles of public beaches. Cameron Parish, for example, is a source point for the U.S. strategic oil reserve, a major portal for the petrochemical industry, a vital link to major ports located in New Orleans, Lake Charles, Houston and Galveston and an anchor for oil and gas maritime repair and service. More than $2.3 billion in Liquefied Natural Gas and related projects are either under construction or on the drawing board in the heart of our service territory, while agriculture and aquaculture enterprises total $41.6 million each year.

Those of us who have lived our entire lives in this sportsman's paradise know that while the region has its rewards both tangible and intangible, it also has its share of challenges. We are intimately familiar with the many factors that threaten the very existence of our homeland. Many of our citizens are fully aware of the fragility of our land and our water and are well-versed in the conditions that have the potential to undermine our way of life. Erosion, storms and storm surge, drought, repeated flooding, saltwater intrusion and even "man-made" disasters such as the BP oil spill of 2010 all threaten the sustainability of our region.

JEFF DAVIS ELECTRIC'S CONCERN WITH "PROPOSED FEDERAL WATER GRABS"

In the interest of fairness, we are mindful of the fact that it was an executive order signed by President Franklin Delano Roosevelt on May 11, 1935, and subsequent Federal action that catalyzed the electric cooperative movement and led to the economic advancement and improved quality of life for millions of rural citizens across the country. And while it's true that rural electrification was sparked by an act of the executive branch of the Federal Government, I would like to point out that the formation of the Rural Electrification Administration did not directly build one rural electric cooperative, nor did it force, mandate or require that one cooperative be constructed; this progressive New Deal initiative simply and appropriately provided those residing in the U.S. countryside a less cumbersome pathway for creating cooperative organizations for themselves, on their own, according to their own vision, in their own communities, to serve their own interests. It was a low-cost loan mechanism made available to privately held, independent, locally controlled power providers. It was, and was intended to be, a public-private partnership in every sense of the term, one that worked best when government provided the proper support and then stepped out of the way to let the local people apply the solutions that made the most sense for their particular circumstances.

We are concerned that the Environmental Protection Agency's proposed Federal water grab goes too far in disturbing a delicate public-private balance by imposing additional unnecessary permitting requirements, adding greater burdens and bureaucratic red tape while further restricting our opportunity to continue economic progress and threatening our cooperative's ability to deliver safe, affordable, reliable electric power to our members. In my opinion, the current rules go beyond far enough.

A prime example of the manner in which overreaching Federal policies have proven problematic and wasteful for our cooperative occurred in the wake of Hurricane Rita nearly 10 years ago. On Sept. 24, 2005, roughly 3 weeks after Hurricane Katrina more famously made landfall on the eastern side of our state, Hurricane Rita struck our coastline in southwest Louisiana, causing $4.7 billion in damage across the region and destroying roughly 40 percent of Jeff Davis Electric's 10,086 accounts along 1,600 miles of electrical power distribution and transmission lines. The storm completely destroyed our branch office located in Cameron, LA, which was established to serve the residents and commercial consumers along the coast. A 5-acre tract of land was generously donated to the cooperative by one of the cooperative's long-time directors, Mr. Charles S. Hackett 25 miles north of Cameron to rebuild the branch office. The current level of Federal oversight through the Clean Water Act caused delays and expenses to the cooperative in the form of environmental surveys, floodplain surveys, permits and inspections that amounted to thousands of dollars being spent before the first shovel of dirt could be turned. During that process, it was discovered that two of the 5 acres were declared wetlands because of the presence of a certain species of indigenous vegetation. This land was farm land that had lain idle for several years because Mr. Hackett no longer wanted to have it farmed. It was not wetlands. Because this certain vegetation was found on the property, according to Federal guidelines, nothing could be done with the land until mitigation took place. In order to take advantage of Mr. Hackett's generosity, Jeff Davis Electric was forced to purchase 2 acres of wetlands from the Federal Government in an unknown location for environmental mitigation. The purchase cost Jeff Davis Electric and its members $30,000. This was an unforeseen expense that had to be passed on to our consumer/members who ultimately bear the cost of unnecessarily burdensome Federal oversight and regulation. Expanding the oversight of the Federal Government would only add to the cost of providing electrical distribution service to our members who already face burdensome regulations and restrictions of use to land which they presently own. Again, this is just one example.

This is the type of burdensome Federal regulation that we need less of, not more. An expansion of the Clean Water Act as currently proposed in the EPA's "Waters of the United States" rule would complicate, not simplify, our Co-op's routine operations and maintenance. The ambiguous definitions in the proposed rule will vastly expand the reach of the Clean Water Act and cause major problems for our customers in Louisiana's coastal plains. For instance, simply performing regular maintenance of our power lines, poles and other infrastructure to ensure reliability for our customers would require additional permitting, additional costs, and unreasonable delays.

We have faced and overcome major challenges as we lie in the direct path of occasional hurricanes. However, under additional Federal regulations as proposed by the EPA, restoring the electrical lifeline to our customers after a similar natural disaster would be much more arduous and perhaps unattainable.

CONCLUSION

It's my personal view and the view of Jeff Davis Electric that the stringent Federal rules and regulations currently in place, in addition to those imposed by state and local authorities, are useful and effective in protecting our wetlands, our precious water resources and our natural habitat. The stringent existing requirements already make it difficult to build infrastructure to new commercial enterprises and adequately maintain right-of-way to ensure cost-effective service reliability for our members.

Again, as a lifelong resident of southwest Louisiana and an avid outdoorsman, I have seen our land besieged by numerous disasters both natural and man-made. And I have also witnessed the resilience of our land and how it has the capacity to renew, reinvigorate and heal itself despite the degree of damage sustained. Major Hurricanes, from Audrey and Andrew to Rita and Ike, have pummeled our coastline over the decades, yet the land and its people continue to stand strong in the face of hardship.

I urge the subcommittee to seriously consider the impact of Federal rules and regulations on the people of southwest Louisiana and members of Jeff Davis Electric, many of whom have spent their entire lives in the wetlands. Our region has benefited greatly from the efforts of the state and Federal Government, as well as private agencies, to protect and preserve our wetlands, and for this we are grateful. However, there is a tipping point where unnecessary mandates and restrictions intended to help our people become punitive and inhibit the ability of our economy to grow and our people to prosper. Any policies adopted by the Federal Government need to be smart and effective in achieving the desired outcome without the negative unintended consequences that diminish the ability of our rural cooperative members to continue their way of life and provide for their families. We prefer to see the Federal Government as a partner in environmental preservation, not a deterrent to progress.

The five Louisiana Parishes served by Jeff Davis Electric

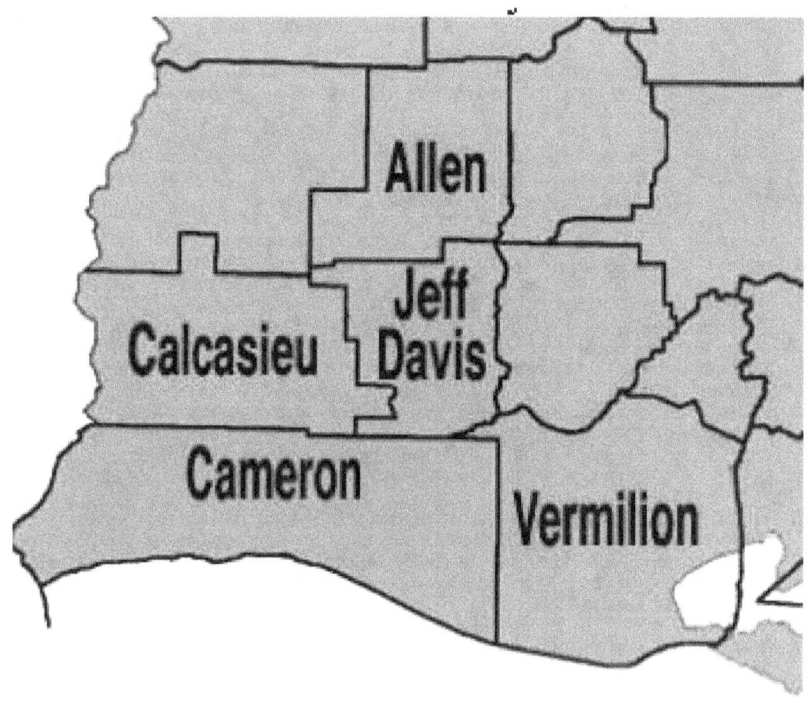

Dr. FLEMING. Thank you, Mr. Heinen. Thank you, panel, for your testimony. At this point we will begin our questions for witnesses.

To allow Members to participate, and to ensure we can hear from all of our witnesses today, Members are limited to 5 minutes for their questions. However, if Members have additional questions, we can have additional rounds of questioning, where Members can submit their questions for the hearing record.

After the Ranking Member and I pose our questions, I will then recognize Members alternatively on both sides of the aisle, in order of seniority. I now recognize myself for 5 minutes.

My first question is for both Mr. Sullivan and Mr. Heinen. The statement was made that the Clean Water Act is not under this committee's jurisdiction, but that is hardly the point. The point is that we have many people who are under our jurisdiction who are being harmed or potentially harmed by what we are talking about here today.

So, here is the question. Everyone shares the goal of having clean water and safe drinking water, but there has been some confusion on the implementation of the Clean Water Act due to two

Supreme Court rulings. The proposed Waters of the U.S. rule purports to clear up this confusion and provide regulatory certainty. Do you think it achieves this purpose?

Mr. Sullivan and Mr. Heinen, do you think that these new regulatory positions that have been taken help clear up that confusion?

Mr. SULLIVAN. No, I think it adds——

Dr. FLEMING. Microphone, please.

Mr. SULLIVAN. No, I think it adds to the confusion. Everything that we have dealt with, starting going back to guidance— guidance, we had some clarification, we thought, from both the Army Corps of Engineers and the EPA, as far as reclamation and recycled water goes. And when it came to the draft rule, there wasn't one thing that they had agreed upon. It was far more draconian and no specificity as to what we were trying to deal with. It just made it unwieldy, and that is——

Dr. FLEMING. So you have seen expansion——

Mr. SULLIVAN. We have seen——

Dr. FLEMING [continuing]. Of powers, of Federal powers, without clarification, perhaps even more vagueness.

Mr. SULLIVAN. Yes, it made it much more vague in what we would try to deal with.

Dr. FLEMING. And you have to deal with the technicalities of these regulations. So you are right there, on the ground, in terms of having to implement these, or abide by these.

Mr. SULLIVAN. On a daily basis.

Dr. FLEMING. Right. OK. Mr. Heinen?

Mr. HEINEN. Plain and simple, until I see it, the final in writing, nothing is clarified, because it changes constantly. We have been dealing with that for many years. So let me see it in writing, let me have a chance to look at it and see what the final ruling is. So—as far as for clarification, there is none.

Dr. FLEMING. Well, we had a hearing on this just a year ago, and both sides of the aisle agreed there need to be clarifications. Have we sent any?

Mr. HEINEN. No.

Dr. FLEMING. OK. Thank you. Now—again, Mr. Heinen—an electric cooperative witness testified last year that it would take longer to permit the building of a new electricity transmission and distribution line than to build it. You testified that your ratepayers had to pay for Clean Water Act mitigation costs that resulted from Hurricane Rita. How will the WOTUS proposal impact new electricity lines built by your cooperative, or built by the Southwestern Power Marketing Administration, which serves some rural utilities in Louisiana?

Mr. HEINEN. Basically, more regulations, more permits, more red tape to deal with adds cost, and cost adds that to the basic consumer at the end of our line, who is already struggling to make ends meet.

Dr. FLEMING. OK. More regulation, more red tape, more cost.

Mr. HEINEN. That is correct.

Dr. FLEMING. Mr. Ogsbury, Mr. Sullivan, Mr. Myrum, and Mr. Heinen, throughout today's testimony we have heard time and again there is confusion as to what some of these proposed regulations could mean at the local level. We have also heard that there is little or no communication prior to the issuance of these proposals, particularly the Forest Service's Groundwater Directive with the states and local governmental entities.

Was there a breakdown in communication between the Federal Government and the state and local governments, and were governments and water and power districts impacted by these proposals? Just quick answers from each of you.

Mr. OGSBURY. Chairman Fleming, Ranking Member Huffman, there was insufficient communication with states during the development of those proposals.

Dr. FLEMING. OK. Mr. Sullivan?

Mr. SULLIVAN. Yes, we didn't learn about it until the last minute, and then there was actually no communication.

Dr. FLEMING. OK. Mr. Myrum?

Mr. MYRUM. Came as a surprise to all of us, I can assure you. And our State Department of Ecology had no idea.

Dr. FLEMING. Mr. Heinen?

Mr. HEINEN. Short answer is yes.

Dr. FLEMING. OK. So, in the last seconds of my questions, I would have to say that this administration is notable for its overreach in many areas, in terms of administration. In fact, the Supreme Court—even decisions as one lopsided as now nine to zero, has shown that this administration has gone way past its authority. And I would just have to say this is just another example of what we are seeing today in the name of clarification.

With that, I yield to the Ranking Member for questions.

Mr. HUFFMAN. Thank you, Mr. Chairman, and thanks to the witnesses.

Professor Buzbee, you talked about the Supreme Court rulings that have clarified, but also added uncertainty to this issue of what constitutes Clean Water Act jurisdiction over various waters. How many different tests do we now have under Supreme Court decisions by different justices that are supposed to tell us the answer of what constitutes the scope of authority under the Clean Water Act?

Mr. BUZBEE. It is difficult to give an exact number. What you have is a unanimous Supreme Court, and *Riverside Bayview Homes* allowed the Federal Government to set the line between land and water and protected what are called adjacent waters.

Then the *Solid Waste Agency Northern Cook County* case— SWANCC, as we all call it—said that protecting isolated waters, due to migratory bird use, was too far. And that had some other language that left things somewhat unclear, which is why the *Rapanos* case ended up so important. And then that case ended up actually splitting three different ways, and the ruling most people think is most important is one by Justice Kennedy that then had a two-pronged analysis that was called for.

So, numerically—and then, to make it more complicated, you actually had two different majorities opining on what waters deserved protection. So you end up having a great deal of confusion, which increases permitting costs, makes it harder for people on the ground, both those who want to use land or want to permit, and those who are trying to act as responsible officials. They all struggle.

Mr. HUFFMAN. Right. Thank you for that. So, I guess I could understand, then, why Mr. Myrum would be concerned about reinterpretation and cycles of interpretation and litigation. But, at the same time, I think his testimony makes a strong case for why we need kind of, once and for all, to resolve all of these chaotic and conflicting interpretations, and have a single standard.

We have a situation where Mr. Heinen was blindsided by the finding that a piece of property was designated a wetland based on a plant being present. Mr. Heinen, wouldn't you agree that it would be far preferable to have a science-based rule that looks at the water connectivity to downstream waters for water quality purposes, rather than have something random, like the presence of a plant, given all this lack of certainty blindside you with a determination?

Mr. HEINEN. It depends on who the scientist is.

Mr. HUFFMAN. Well——

Mr. HEINEN. It is interpretation. A lot of people say that particular plant can only be in wetlands. A scientist has said that.

Mr. HUFFMAN. Yes.

Mr. HEINEN. That is not the case in my——

Mr. HUFFMAN. Wouldn't you like to know what that means, though, so as a piece of property might be——

Mr. HEINEN. Clarification would be nice, yes——

Mr. HUFFMAN [continuing]. Given to you, you would know?

Mr. HEINEN. Clarification would be nice. Yes, I agree.

Mr. HUFFMAN. It seems to me that some of this comes down to getting the final rule and reading it, and seeing if it says what officials from the administration have been promising us it will say.

So, Mr. Sullivan, to your point—and I want to commend you for your water recycling, by the way. We are going to need a lot more of that to get through the summer ahead of us. So thank you for your leadership there. But you are concerned that you haven't yet seen anything in writing that would address your concerns about water recycling.

I am aware, though, that the Administration has said as recently as a couple of months ago that they are working to define these things, that they are committed to making sure that the final rule—in fact, I will quote Director McCarthy—''You will have my assurance that these things that have never been in before, that we have never talked about, will not be in the final rule.'' She is talking about water re-use and recycling facilities.

So, assuming she does what she says she is going to do, would that not address your concern about water recycling?

Mr. SULLIVAN. Well, I think our concern is we don't know what she is going to do.

Mr. HUFFMAN. Well, she has told you what she is going to do.

Mr. SULLIVAN. No, she—there is no clarification to that. We did that in guidance, and that didn't work. And when it got to the rule—we don't know what the final rule—the draft rule didn't specify anything, wasn't clear, was ambiguous, and would create some concern. So, when the rule comes out, we would hope—if the rule comes out, and to maybe satisfy everybody—that there be at least a 60-day final comment period, so that people could address it.

There is no one here that is against the Clean Water Act. It is how much further you are going to go with it——

Mr. HUFFMAN. Fair enough.

Mr. SULLIVAN [continuing]. That doesn't guarantee anything.

Mr. HUFFMAN. I just want to wrap up with Mr. Ogsbury. Thanks for your testimony on behalf of the Western Governors. And I hear you loud and clear when you want to make sure that states have primacy when it comes to the allocation and administration of water. And I know that, in the past, the Western Governors have extended that position to legislation proposed in Congress that would preempt state water law—for example, in California.

But I did not see a position by the Western Governors bill on a sweeping preemptive bill proposed by Mr. Valadao and others last year that would have preempted California water rights. The state of California vehemently opposed it. I am assuming that this position, though, remains constant, that you continue to oppose preemptive Federal acts on water that interfere with state primacy on water allocation, water rights, water management.

Mr. OGSBURY. Chairman Fleming, Ranking Member Huffman, members of the subcommittee, I would submit that the statement in the Governors' resolution that I recited before speaks for itself on the Governors' commitment to state primacy over water resources.

Mr. HUFFMAN. Thank you.

Dr. FLEMING. The gentleman yields. The Chair recognizes Dr. Gosar for 5 minutes.

Dr. GOSAR. Thank you very much, Mr. Chairman.

Supervisor Sullivan, it is good to see you again.

Mr. SULLIVAN. Thank you.

Dr. GOSAR. Now, you testified that the National Water Resources Association is concerned that the proposed WOTUS rule will make it more difficult to meet water needs. Given the historic drought and other challenges we have in the West, can you elaborate a little more about why that is so concerning? I mean, particularly from your state and my state next door—the state of Arizona?

Mr. SULLIVAN. Sure. We just believe that, because there is no specificity, what we are asking for here, that it makes it much more difficult for us to put in a new project, to create new water supply. And we have enough hoops to go through right now that is in compliance with the Clean Water Act. We don't know why we are trying to add to it, because this, to us, looks like we are adding to the requirements.

Dr. GOSAR. Now, you made a question that NWRA members would prefer to invest their public funds in infrastructure and environmental enhancements, rather than litigation. That is a great point. How concerned are you that the vagueness in WOTUS will lead to your members wasting considerable amounts of money on frivolous lawsuits?

Mr. SULLIVAN. Right now we are dealing with one small group that is suing our district over the Clean Water Act. This particular group has about 130 lawsuits, starting in northern California, and now they are working their way down to southern California. It is a money grab and we are going to stand up on this one, because we don't believe that we are violating anything within the Clean

Water Act. And because the Clean Water Act is not specific, it is wide open, it is hunting season for any attorney that would like to come in and take our money.

Dr. GOSAR. So you also testified that you were very concerned that WOTUS would make groundwater jurisdictional. Even EPA Administrator McCarthy testified a couple of months ago that the rule was so vague it could apply to groundwater. I mean in her own words.

Can you elaborate on why this is such a concern for the Ag community and private water users?

Mr. SULLIVAN. Sure. We believe that, actually, everybody—especially in our agricultural areas, everybody is actually the steward of their own environment. And I think that we have had a pretty good chance, or pretty good opportunity, at this time to prove ourselves. We have been able to expand our agricultural uses through the use of reclaimed water. And part of that came through some grants from the Bureau of Reclamation. I mean we have been able to do a lot.

Dr. GOSAR. Mr. Buzbee, with so many directives out there that—there are so many, it is just a myriad, it is mind-boggling. Don't you think that the agency should work with Congress to make sure that its intent is right?

Mr. BUZBEE. Certainly, I think the agency should always be respectful of Congress and work with it. But, at the same time, an agency has to abide by the law as enacted.

Dr. GOSAR. Well, we are really interpreting it beyond the scope of what was intended.

Mr. BUZBEE. I don't believe so. And I think that we have, at this point, the Supreme Court and the three decisions have certainly left uncertainty where there had been certainty for three decades. But there really was a bipartisan, very stable period where, for three decades through the Reagan administration, there was a consensus on what was protected, and why, and how it should be protected, and those regulations barely changed.

We still have the same Clean Water Act today, and I think, my sense is these regulations are—especially with the science report—really bring a lot of clarity. Someone who now has a piece of land is trying to figure out how they would be dealt with, you have the connectivity report, which I think—being over 400 pages long, and I assume the final regulations will, as with the draft, connect the two together, and people will have a much firmer sense of what is required.

Dr. GOSAR. Director Ogsbury, would you agree on that conversation, that Congress should be consulted in regards to the new directives on WOTUS before pursuing?

Mr. OGSBURY. I certainly agree that, because states have primacy with respect to management of water resources, that states should be consulted at the very front end.

Dr. GOSAR. Supervisor Sullivan, how about you? I mean you see this from the application from time and on the ground. Would you agree that Congress should be part of this rulemaking process, engaged properly, to see if it is germane as to the application?

Mr. SULLIVAN. Absolutely. I think that is where the representation of the people and the local elected officials reside, whether it is from local government, state government, up to the Congress. And I believe that that is where the laws should be made, and should not, and that is where we ought to listen to it.

Dr. GOSAR. So, one last point. The narrative that we heard from the rulemaking process was crystal clear.

Mr. SULLIVAN. No.

Dr. GOSAR. That is what I thought. Thank you.

Dr. FLEMING. The gentleman yields. The Chair recognizes Mrs. Napolitano for 5 minutes.

Mrs. NAPOLITANO. Thank you, Mr. Chairman. And welcome to the witnesses.

I would like to, first off, introduce two letters to the record, one dated November 14th, last year and one November 5th. One is from the California Water Board, the other one is from CASA, the California Association of Sanitation Agencies. Water Board says that they strongly support the agency's intent to adopt regs to provide clarity. That is what we are all asking for, is clarity. Comprehensive rulemaking represents a major improvement over status quo.

The second letter says it does not—they also endorse a proposed rule clarification that the agencies do not intend to alter the regulation of groundwater at the Federal level. In fact, proposed rule codifies a number of waters and features. The agencies have a long-standing practice, generally considered not to be Waters of the United States.

Now, both EPA and Army Corps fall under the jurisdiction of Transportation, of which I am the Ranking Member. And we have just recently held a hearing with Ms. McCarthy, and we asked repeatedly the same questions you are being asked today. And she has stated unequivocally that should there be questions after the final rule—and, by the way, there were over a million responses. Of course, a lot of them were duplicates. But the comment period was for 207 days. Did any of you reply? Did you submit any comments during that period, any of you?

Mr. SULLIVAN. Yes, we did supply a lot of comments. And just so that you know, there basically were 216 water districts that replied with comments. They are all large water districts. There are 14 storm water associations that——

Mrs. NAPOLITANO. OK, I get that. I understand that. But I wanted to know, because I don't remember any one of you coming to me and talking to me about it, either. Have you?

Mr. SULLIVAN. I believe that we did.

Mrs. NAPOLITANO. When?

Mr. SULLIVAN. It was in last October, November.

Mrs. NAPOLITANO. All right. But I was not the Ranking Member then on Transportation, sir. So that makes a little bit more of a difference. And being able to understand the questions that you bring up that we can then take into consideration and ask those agencies to clarify, to be able to help us be able to be effective.

Second, I understand that the rule will be clarified, what, some time before summer. Then it will be more comment period, I understand. Or at least I hope there will be. What are we looking at, in terms of being able to bring before this body, or the Transportation

Subcommittee, to be able to have information so, when you see the final rule, what is it that we need to work with?

Because in some instances—and Ms. McCarthy was requested— why was there a difference between region's interpretation of the application of the different rules or regulations? There are problems. We know that. She knows that. Why are we not dealing with those, instead of bringing to the forefront, and dealing at the local level, or directly with that chief of theirs, to be able to clarify and make sure that we understand that she gets to those individuals and brings them to the forefront or up to speed into what they need to do?

[No response.]

Mrs. NAPOLITANO. I mean, we can argue that unless we change that, we are not going to have the quality across—for the implementation of what should be to protect our waters.

Comment, anybody?

[No response.]

Mrs. NAPOLITANO. None?

Mr. OGSBURY. Chairman Fleming, Ranking Member Huffman, Congresswoman Napolitano, members of the committee, we would be happy to provide all of WGA's comments on the proposed rule to the subcommittee and to you, individually.

Mrs. NAPOLITANO. Well, that would be nice. I don't want tomes. I would like just a synopsis.

[Laughter.]

Mrs. NAPOLITANO. We have enough reading, thank you very much.

But in order for us to understand what your issues are, we need to be able to have our staff to be able to clarify where you are coming from, so then we can be more specific about where we need to go with them. And I would love to have them come to our districts. And maybe my—I have a son living near you, and near Lake Elsinore.

Mr. OGSBURY. Right.

Mrs. NAPOLITANO. I understand the issue that you have in those areas. But we also have issues in all of southern California with water. So we all are interested in making sure that the agencies, all of them, work with us to be able to address some of the things that we all need to work on, regardless. Water is water. It is life, it is business, it is economy. So I would be more than happy to later talk to any of you.

Thank you, Mr. Chair.

Dr. FLEMING. The gentlelady yields back. The Chair recognizes Mr. McClintock for 5 minutes.

Mr. McCLINTOCK. Thank you, Mr. Chairman. I would like to begin by once again gently correcting my friend from California, who once again in this subcommittee has asserted that the Valadao legislation preempted California water rights. It did exactly the opposite, as has been explained to him time and again.

Mr. HUFFMAN. Would the gentleman yield?

Mr. McCLINTOCK. Not yet. It protected California water rights from any encroachments, whether by Federal or state authorities. It was this provision that actually strengthened those rights. It was supported by the Northern California Water Association, representing the senior water rights holders.

The assertion of vastly expanded Federal jurisdiction over our waters I find particularly terrifying at a time when we are in the midst, in California, of not only the worst drought in recorded history, hydrologists are telling us it could be the worst drought in the last 1,200 years. Our snow pack is at 6 percent of normal. Our reservoirs are, many of them are nearing empty.

The New Melones Reservoir is currently at 22 percent of capacity. And yet, this week the Bureau of Reclamation is spilling 30,000 acre-feet of water—that is 10 billion gallons of water—in order to encourage steelhead trout to migrate to the ocean, which they generally tend to do without our helpful assistance. Ten billion gallons is enough to meet the annual residential needs of a population of about 300,000 people at a time when we are at the end of the rainy season, there is virtually no snow left in the mountains, and our reservoirs are becoming nearly depleted.

And now we have a proposal by the Administration to vastly increase Federal jurisdiction over these waters. Mr. Myrum, Mr. Sullivan, I know why that terrifies me. What are your thoughts on the subject?

Mr. SULLIVAN. Up to you, Tom.

[Laughter.]

Mr. MYRUM. Well, I——

Mr. SULLIVAN. I talked enough. No, it terrifies us that we still have a lot of drought-supported water supply to take care of. To put additional regulations in front of us to create new water and to bring water from different areas makes it very difficult for us to sustain something if this drought lasts another couple of years.

So, to have this rule be established when we are struggling with a water supply at this point—and I don't know of anybody in my area or most of them in California that have any problem with clean water right now. They can turn on the tap, and they get water, and it is clean.

Mr. MCCLINTOCK. Well, the point I am trying to get at is there seems to be a complete lack of simple common sense in the Federal Government's approach to these water issues. Have you seen that in your jurisdiction? And is that one of the reasons why you might be reluctant to see the Federal Government assert even more authority?

Mr. SULLIVAN. Yes, the simple answer is absolutely. We had our experience from guidance, and then from guidance it went to the rule. And from guidance to the rule it was far expanded. That is what worries us.

Mr. MCCLINTOCK. Well, as you know, the Bureau of Reclamation was supposed to be here today, but refused to join us. In a 2008 excerpt from an Interior Department letter on the Clean Water Act jurisdictional issue, they had written, "In general, Reclamation has particular interest in Clean Water Act jurisdictional issues. Indeed, Reclamation and its project beneficiaries are in need of guidance to better understand when or whether its dams and irrigation facilities, including ditches, canals, arroyos, and other water delivery channels and works—collectively referred to as ditches—are considered jurisdictional waters, subject to regulation by the Army Corps of Engineers, and the Environmental Protection Act under the CWA, or as tributaries to such waters. Likewise, Reclamation has an interest in understanding when waters adjacent to these facilities are jurisdictional, and when discharges into or from those facilities are subject to CWA jurisdiction and attendant permitting requirements.''

It is interesting, because Reclamation says that it submitted testimony that it is satisfied that their facilities, including ditches, are not covered by the Waters of the U.S. proposal. Do you agree? Mr. Sullivan?

Mr. SULLIVAN. Yes, we would agree.

Mr. MCCLINTOCK. Mr. Mauck, is that your understanding, as well?

Mr. MAUCK. I am sorry, I am not familiar with the Bureau of Reclamation and those statements. I am here to testify about my experience as a Clear Creek County Commissioner——

Mr. MCCLINTOCK. I see, I am sorry. How about Mr. Myrum?

Mr. MYRUM. I understand the Bureau of Reclamation has an interest in the jurisdiction of the Clean Water Act over their facilities. As I mentioned during my testimony, the Clean Water Act has exercised jurisdiction over our facilities, either through Federal court decisions, or in some unintended ways. And the Bureau has not stepped up to try to counter that.

I did mention the regulatory guidance letter, where they were a particular help, and that is nice. But they could do more. It would have been nice to see them here today to show their concern for our facilities, at least as much concern as we have.

Mr. MCCLINTOCK. Thank you.

Dr. FLEMING. OK. The gentleman's time is up. The Chair now recognizes Mrs. Lummis for 5 minutes.

Mrs. LUMMIS. Thank you, Mr. Chairman. Mr. Ogsbury, is California part of the Western Governors' Association?

Mr. OGSBURY. Chairman Fleming, Ranking Member Huffman, Congresswoman Lummis, yes, it is.

Mrs. LUMMIS. Did California dissent from the position of the Western Governors' Association?

Mr. OGSBURY. With respect to adoption of that resolution, it is a resolution that reflects the collective voice of the Western Governors. The individual votes are not disclosed, and I am not exactly sure what that might have been, anyway.

Mrs. LUMMIS. OK, thank you. Mr. Ogsbury, who determines how much groundwater can be withdrawn from a state's borders, the state or the Federal Government?

Mr. OGSBURY. Chairman Fleming, Ranking Member Huffman, Congresswoman Lummis, members of the committee, that would be the state.

Mrs. LUMMIS. Well, while the Federal Government can have reserved surface water rights on Federal lands—back in my day we used to call that the Winters Doctrine. Is it still called the Winters Doctrine, by the way? Does anybody know?

Mr. OGSBURY. Sure.

Mrs. LUMMIS. OK, good. Well, I am not that dated, then.

[Laughter.]

Mrs. LUMMIS. And no comments from the peanut gallery on that.

Can the Federal Government have reserved rights in ground-water? Mr. Ogsbury?

Mr. OGSBURY. Chairman Fleming, Ranking Member Huffman, Congresswoman Lummis, no——

Mrs. LUMMIS. That is what states do.

Mr. OGSBURY [continuing]. Statutory Act of Congress, no Federal appellate court has ever held that Federal reserves—have upheld Federal reserve rights to groundwater.

Mrs. LUMMIS. By the states? So the Federal Government cannot have reserved water rights in groundwater, reserved water rights? Not surface water rights. Reserved water rights in groundwater?

Mr. OGSBURY. No Act of Congress or decision of the court, of a Federal appeals court has so held.

Mrs. LUMMIS. Do you believe that the groundwater directive shifts groundwater authority away from states and to the Federal Government?

Mr. OGSBURY. I believe that our comments on that directive reflected a concern that certain provisions of the directive could be interpreted to erode state authority. Fortunately, we are very pleased that the Forest Service has stopped its work on that rule, on that directive.

Mrs. LUMMIS. If there is a shift in authority, could it lead to litigation, regulatory uncertainty?

Mr. OGSBURY. Again, I would hope that the question is academic. I would like to take the Forest Service on its word that they have stopped work on this directive, and if they reinitiate such a directive, they will start from the top and consult states at the very front end. But, yes, if there were a shift in authority, then there is certainly potential for more regulatory confusion, more litigation.

Mrs. LUMMIS. Thank you. Question for Mr. Sullivan. Is it correct to say that the Bureau of Reclamation has invested taxpayer dollars into your agency's water recycling and groundwater recharge projects?

Mr. SULLIVAN. Absolutely.

Mrs. LUMMIS. Mr. Myrum, has the Bureau of Rec made investments in Washington State? And could it make investments in new storage at a later point?

Mr. MYRUM. They have made significant investments in Washington State. We have major projects. And they are in the process of developing a project for our new storage in the Yakima Valley, which we certainly hope they will contribute to that cause.

Mrs. LUMMIS. Now, for both of you, would these investments be impacted if the Forest Service's Groundwater Directive went forward, as well as the Waters of the U.S. proposal? I will start with you, Mr. Myrum.

Mr. MYRUM. Well, thank you. Ma'am, absolutely, they would be impacted.

Let's start with the groundwater. If you take the groundwater through the Forest Service and the reserved water rights, that water, subsurface, is already flowing toward a river. But specifically, the Yakima Basin, uses a system called Total Water Supply Available. It would then be taking water out of that Total Water Supply Available in that system for their own needs, and they would be very much a junior appropriator under a fully adjudicated system. So they would interrupt that process. So, if we are doing new storage, then the ability to get water for new storage could be an issue.

The Waters of the United States rule is really an issue related to the construction of new facilities. A programmatic EIS has been done in the Yakima, and now the individual projects within that are starting to be constructed. If there are new jurisdictional waters after the fact that now have to be considered through the NEPA process, it could turn it back several years, if not change the result all together.

So that is an example of some of the uncertainty that we have mentioned earlier.

Mrs. LUMMIS. Thank you. Mr. Chairman, I yield back.

Dr. FLEMING. Mr. LaMalfa is recognized for 5 minutes.

Mr. LAMALFA. Thank you, Mr. Chairman. I have a tip from a colleague from California, from Mr. Huffman, about having difficulty with the one boot. I recommend two. I move around here pretty good with that.

[Laughter.]

Mr. LAMALFA. All right. I tease my colleague from the West.

So to Mr. Heinen here again, just following up on the issue with power lines and that right-of-way, et cetera, of course, this is something we are trying to accomplish in northern California, as well. What will this do for the reliability of the grid, do you think, with this rule in place? You already mentioned it will raise cost, and the red tape of getting it done. How does that help with grid reliability?

Then also, what do you see it actually doing in the bottom line for water quality, to have to go through this extra level of regulation and permitting? Is there actually a help to water quality?

Mr. HEINEN. In my opinion, no. There would be no difference in water quality from what it is now. As far as reliability, any time you extend the process of maintaining and repairing your distribution, your transmission lines, it takes time, adds cost. And when the lights go out and reliability is not what it used to be, believe me, nobody cares about anything else but getting them back on.

Mr. LAMALFA. My understanding that if the rule goes through—which is, indeed, just a rule, we haven't had a whole lot of say in the Congress about if it happens—it would require every crossing of some type of an interpretation of a waterway to pass a litmus test of whether or not it qualifies as a waterway.

So, how do you see that contributing to a timeliness or a cost effectiveness of accomplishing a project?

Mr. HEINEN. Being from southwest Louisiana, and every place you have there is water, that would be very disastrous for us.

Mr. LAMALFA. Mr. Sullivan, talking about recycled water for a moment, again, that is something that many of my colleagues in agriculture do. We don't let water out at the end of the field on our own created irrigation and drainage ditches when we are using water—or if we at least have that power to.

EPA has indicated products could be exempted, but will they? Because it is also being seen that the district is jurisdictional under the Clean Water Act. So which is it?

Mr. SULLIVAN. That is our concern, because most all of our facilities are either adjacent or close to jurisdictional properties. And 60 percent of our reclaimed water goes to Ag. And it has been a really nice agreement with the Ag people, so that they do not pump high-quality groundwater, and that they use the reclaimed water. They have come to rely on it, because it also contains about a bag-and-a-half of fertilizer, hydrogen phosphorous.

So, we have a significant investment in our reclaimed water system, recycled water system, and a lot of that is due to some money from the Bureau of Reclamation.

Mr. LAMALFA. So we are talking in California—when we are looking at much more need for water supply, one way or the other, whether it is recycling, conservation, or water storage, does this proposal help to foment the expedited or even the ability at all to build and expand these types of facilities?

Mr. SULLIVAN. No. In our humble opinion, it makes it much more difficult for us to create new water supplies, because the hoops you are going to have to go through will be incredible.

Mr. LAMALFA. I guess, from my own experience from talking to people around northern California in the farming and ranching, et cetera, is that this isn't some kind of a straw dog that isn't happening. It is already happening, where I have had ranchers comment where they simply re-leveled their property, where they are controlling the water that runs on to and off their water that they irrigate with, that one farmer had to wait 3 years while somebody scared them to death with the idea they were going to bring charges against them.

Another one, not too far away, actually did get 6-digit fines, because they changed their land that had been farmed to wheat before, to grazing for a while, and to olives, I believe. And now have been hit with gigantic fines for using their property as they see fit, that they have owned and operated for generations.

This is something that is already going on. This isn't simply something that is being dreamed up, or some kind of anti-administration thing. This cuts across all political lines, and is something, indeed, that I think is beyond the power of an agency without congressional input. So this is why we have this hearing, and these are just a couple of the anecdotes that we will be seeing of an overreach that goes way beyond anybody's intention for when the Clean Water Act would have been passed many years ago.

But, Mr. Chairman, I appreciate the opportunity to have this panel, these questions. I will yield back.

Dr. FLEMING. The gentleman yields back. Mr. Zinke is recognized for 5 minutes.

Mr. ZINKE. Thank you, Mr. Chairman. And, gentlemen, thank you for being here. I know your time is precious.

There is a saying in Montana that whiskey is for drinking and water is for fighting. And Montana water—we have over 170,000 miles of rivers and streams. And we rely on our water for commodities, for recreation, for energy. And most businesses, most families, and the future of Montana is predicated on water.

We have seen recent EPA rules that just don't make sense. For instance, in a little town like Eureka, Montana, where they are asked to filter the system, and they take it out of the river, where the discharge is now cleaner than the intake. We have seen where little towns like Winnett, Montana were on storm drains because Montana isn't New York City. And we get our water from point sources, we don't get it from the tap or spigot. And generally, on discharge, it does not go into a municipal system. It goes into holding ponds that is appropriate in a state that is the size of from Washington, DC to Chicago, plus 2 miles.

And it seems that the one-size-fits-all approach oftentimes either neglects, overlooks, or is not in the best interest to rural America, particularly Montana. And oftentimes these rules, like this one, is viewed, at least from our state, as by bureaucrats that don't know the difference between Billings, Bozeman, and the Bayou. And there is a big difference between Bozeman and Billings. And I was just down in the Bayou, and I like that area, too.

But where I am leading to is that this one-size-fits-all, what did Montana do? Did we violate something? Because the last time I looked, when the water leaves the great state of Montana from North Dakota or Idaho, it is pretty clean. And my concern is that every cow pond is going to be regulated like the Hudson, and the view from the Potomac is a lot different than the view from Yellowstone.

So, I guess, for Mr. Ogsbury, that you are the Governor. Is there something that Montana did wrong that was justified, changing our groundwater, the way we handle our groundwater? Because I think everyone in this room appreciates clean water.

Mr. OGSBURY. Chairman Fleming, Ranking Member Huffman, Congressman Zinke, members of the committee, Governors have certainly expressed concerns about a one-size-fits-all approach to Federal regulatory activity, as well. And that, I think, is what informs, or what largely informs, their position, that they should be consulted early in the process, so they could better sensitize the regulatory agencies to the hydrological differences, the differences in legal framework, and the different citizen needs that the Governors might have a little more command of.

Mr. ZINKE. And a follow-up question. It seems there is confusion about what this set of rules really mean. There is confusion in this body, there is confusion within different sides. There is confusion in the definitions. And it seems to me there is a breakdown. Because in Montana there is a confusion between the cattlemen, there is confusion between the Ag guys. There is confusion with the recreational guys, and there is confusion—again, this body.

So, was there a breakdown in lack of coordination at the local, the state, the Federal level? Do we need to send it back to where we can start coordinating it again? Because it seems to me there is a broad breadth of definitions that is not uniform. Is there——

Mr. OGSBURY. Chairman Fleming, Ranking Member Huffman, Congressman Zinke, members of the subcommittee, we do believe that consultation with states was inadequate, that states really should be treated more as authentic and equal partners in the development of a proposal that so directly impacts state authority.

I think Governors recognize that they are more than stakeholders, that they have regulatory authorities, constitutional responsibilities, and delegated responsibilities that bear special consideration.

Mr. ZINKE. Thank you, Mr. Chairman. I yield the remaining time. Thank you, sir.

Dr. FLEMING. The gentleman yields back. Mr. Tipton is recognized for 5 minutes.

Mr. TIPTON. Thank you, Mr. Chairman. And just to clarify for my colleague from Montana, I think the origination of "whiskey is for drinking and water is for fighting" started in Colorado.

[Laughter.]

Mr. TIPTON. But, as Westerners, we do stand on common ground, that state law ought to be respected. Water is a private property right. Our priority-based systems ought to be respected by the Federal Government, as well.

And, Chairman Fleming, I thank you for holding this hearing today and shining light on a very important topic.

In recent years, the Federal Government has repeatedly attempted to circumvent long-established state water law in order to hijack water rights. These efforts constitute a gross Federal overreach in violation of private property rights. On multiple fronts, the U.S. Forest Service and other Federal land management agencies are currently attempting to ignore state law and take private water rights, despite objections from elected officials, business owners, and private property advocates.

For example, the Federal Forest Service attempted to implement a process that requires the transfer of privately held water rights to the Federal Government as a permit condition on national forest lands, while offering no compensation for the transfer of these privately held water rights, despite the fact that many stakeholders have invested millions of their own capital in developing those rights.

Although the Forest Service has announced its intention not to require transfer of ownership of water rights to ski areas special use permits outside the ski area permit context, the agency is keeping the policy on the books that requires permittees to transfer their water rights to the U.S., and apply for new water rights in the name of the U.S.

These same nefarious tactics have been used in attempts to hijack private-held water rights associated with agricultural production in the heart of rural America, where farmers, ranchers rely on these rights to secure loans, as well as irrigate crops and livestock. This Federal water grab has brought implications that have begun to extend beyond recreation and farming and ranching communities, and are now threatening municipalities and businesses, as well.

Furthermore, the Forest Service recently proposed the groundwater directive which would have expanded the agency's reach over the groundwater, and established new bureaucratic hurdles to interfere with private water users' ability to access their water.

Make no mistake. The Forest Service seeks to further federalize water resources, erode state authority, and pave the way for unilateral mandates on state water resources, while overriding decades of longstanding policy that the states and the states alone hold jurisdiction over their own groundwater.

Despite statements by Chief Tidwell that the agency is, for the time being, backing off its controversial groundwater directive,

Chief Tidwell offered no guarantees that the directive, or something similar, will not be back in the future. In fact, Chief Tidwell noted that the agency still intends to move forward with it in some form, after gathering more input.

The need for permanent legislative solutions to be able to protect private water rights from Federal takings and interference cannot be overstated. For these reasons, I am reintroducing the Water Rights Protection Act, which passed through the House of Representatives with bipartisan support, and out of this committee with bipartisan support in the last Congress.

The Water Rights Protection Act would protect communities, businesses, recreation opportunities, farmers, ranchers, as well as other individuals that rely on privately held water rights for their livelihood from Federal takings. It would do so by prohibiting the Federal agencies from extorting water rights through the use of permits and leases and other land management arrangements for which it would otherwise have to pay just compensation under the Fifth Amendment of the Constitution.

The bill also prohibits the implementation of the groundwater resource management directive recently promulgated by the Forest Service, as well as any similar directives or regulations they may consider in the future.

The Water Rights Protection Act has already received the endorsements of the National Ski Areas Association, the American Farm Bureau, the National Cattlemen's Beef Association, the Family Farm Alliance, the Public Lands Council, and Club 20. And more groups continue to add to that support, as well.

Mr. Ogsbury, is water a private property right in the West?

Mr. OGSBURY. States, as I understand it, control the allocation of water rights. I am not the subject matter expert, and I would ask the committee's indulgence and permission to provide a more thoughtful answer for the record.

Mr. TIPTON. Well, I would certainly appreciate that. Since 1876, when Colorado became a state, the Federal Government has respected Colorado State law, Western State law, private property rights, our priority-based systems. But now we are continuing this—I have listened to the answers that you, on the panel, have given. Is it your sense, sir, that we are actually seeing the Federal Government trying to find a solution for a problem that they have apparently not strictly identified?

Mr. OGSBURY. Chairman Fleming, Ranking Member Huffman, Congressman Tipton, we certainly think that there is ambiguity in all of the proposals that have been the subject of today's discussion, and we actually would want to work more closely with those Federal agencies to better inform their policy proposals.

Mr. TIPTON. You know, the National Governors Association—I think the comment was—and I—does this concern you? When we are seeing the Federal Government now—under state law, private property rights, state water law, now trying to define states as potentially affected parties, does this seem to you to be a complete disregard of state law that has been respected?

Mr. OGSBURY. Chairman Fleming, Ranking Member Huffman, Congressman Tipton, we certainly feel that we are more than potentially affected parties.

Mr. TIPTON. Thank you, sir. And I yield back. Thank you for your indulgence, Mr. Chairman.

Dr. FLEMING. Yes, gentleman yields back. I want to thank the panel for your valuable testimony and answering questions. We could easily go another couple of hours, but we are not going to do that to you.

[Laughter.]

Dr. FLEMING. Because we have another panel. But I want to thank you. And we may provide more questions in writing, and we appreciate a written response, as well.

And, once again, thank you. And I thank my friend from Louisiana, Mr. Heinen.

You are excused. And our second panel, our panelist, our one panelist, should step forward.

[Pause.]

Dr. FLEMING. We will now hear from our second panel witness. We are joined by Ms. Leslie Weldon, Deputy Chief of the U.S. Forest Service, based in Washington, DC.

I would again like to express my disappointment and frustration that the Bureau of Reclamation was not willing to provide our committee with a witness for proper questioning.

Deputy Chief Weldon, I would like to remind you that your complete written testimony will appear in the hearing record. And I ask that you keep your oral statement to 5 minutes.

As a reminder, when you speak, our clerk will start the timer: the green for 5 minutes—excuse me, 4 minutes, and then yellow for a minute, and then red concludes your remarks.

And certainly, everything will be submitted in the record. So if you don't get everything in, it will certainly be on the record.

So I now recognize Deputy Chief Weldon to testify for 5 minutes.

STATEMENT OF LESLIE WELDON, DEPUTY CHIEF, U.S. FOREST SERVICE, WASHINGTON, DC

Ms. WELDON. Thank you, Chairman Fleming, Ranking Member Huffman, and members of the subcommittee. And thanks for the opportunity to provide perspective on the role of the U.S. Department of Agriculture in the stewardship of water resources on the national forests and national forest system lands.

I was asked to address concerns related to proposed water clauses for ski area permits, and the groundwater directive. Neither of these proposals are directly connected to the proposed rule under the Clean Water Act by the U.S. Army of Corps of Engineers and the EPA.

Let me begin by emphasizing the sole interest of the Forest Service regarding the stewardship of water resources is to help ensure that abundant, clean water is available now and into the future. Whether it is to ensure reliable drinking water for communities, abundant flows for agriculture, to sustain domestic animals, as well as wildlife and fish population, or to make snow for skiing and other world class recreation, everything is done with an eye for the broad public interest, and in recognition of the critical role that national forests play as a vital source of water.

In June of 2014, a notice of proposed ski area water clauses for the agency's Special Uses Handbook was published in the Federal

Register. These clauses are intended to ensure the long-term availability of water for ski area operations without requiring Federal ownership of water rights associated with ski areas operating on national forest system lands by making sufficiency of water a requirement of the permit holder. We believe that the final clauses will ensure that ski areas have sufficient water to continue to be able to provide recreation opportunities to the public, and economic support to the communities that depend on their revenue, while addressing the concern of not inhibiting market forces associated with water resources.

Since publishing our proposed groundwater directive in May of 2014, and after 150 days of comments, several hearings, letters, and many conversations, we have heard loudly and clearly the concerns of both the content and our approach to the directive. Recognizing the importance of the need for full transparency, and for close coordination with other jurisdictions and stakeholders, we are not moving forward with a proposal at this time.

Rather, we have shifted our efforts to actively engaging in a productive and collaborative dialog with states, tribes, and other stakeholders to develop a new proposal that will better protect against groundwater contamination, improve environmental analysis, reduce uncertainty and costs associated with potential litigation, and increase efficient use and conservation of groundwater. This will take time.

We recognize that there is still much work to be done, and are committed to a transparent, collaborative, and cooperative approach to meet our shared stewardship responsibilities for groundwater-dependent resources on national forest system lands.

Last December, Chief Tidwell issued a letter to regional foresters, directing them to engage with their State Governors to address their concerns. The agency is also working with the Western States Water Council to develop better policy. In fact, we are meeting with the Council later this week. These discussions have been positive and fruitful. We look forward to continuing this work, and will not move a new proposal until we have successfully engaged with states, tribes, and other interests, including working closely with Congress.

On behalf of the Forest Service, I emphasize that nothing in the implementation of our stewardship responsibilities of national forest and grasslands will infringe on state authority for water allocation and state and tribal authority for water quality protection. As a direct result of the public will and congressional intent, the national forest system today provides sources of clean drinking water for people in more than 3,400 communities in 42 states and the Commonwealth of Puerto Rico. It is our goal that, in partnership with the states, tribes, and all water users, these resources remain abundant and clean for present and future generations. We will work with you on the direction that accomplishes just that.

And I thank you for the opportunity to be here today, and welcome any questions. Thank you.

[The prepared statement of Ms. Weldon follows:]

PREPARED STATEMENT OF LESLIE WELDON, DEPUTY CHIEF, NATIONAL FOREST SYSTEM, U.S. DEPARTMENT OF AGRICULTURE FOREST SYSTEM

Chairman Fleming, Ranking Member Huffman, and members of the subcommittee, thank you for the opportunity to provide perspective on the role of the U.S. Department of Agriculture (USDA) in the stewardship of water resources on National Forest System (NFS) lands. Specifically, USDA has been asked to respond to concerns related to proposed ski area water clauses and a proposed groundwater directive, neither of which has any relationship to the proposed rule under the Clean Water Act by the U.S. Army Corps of Engineers and U.S. Environmental Protection Agency.

SKI AREA WATER CLAUSES

On June 23, 2014, notice of proposed ski area water clauses for the agency's Special Uses Handbook was published in the Federal Register. These clauses are intended to ensure the long-term availability of water for ski area operations without requiring Federal ownership of the water rights associated with ski areas operating on NFS lands. The Forest Service received nearly 13,000 comments in response to the proposal, of which 35 were unique. We are evaluating the comments and considering proposed revisions to the clauses. We believe the final clauses will provide for sufficiency of water, while addressing the concern of not inhibiting market forces associated with water resources. The intent will be to make sufficiency of water a requirement of the permit holder. We believe that the final clauses will ensure that ski areas have sufficient water to continue to be able to provide recreation opportunities to the public and economic support to the communities that depend on their revenue.

PROPOSED GROUNDWATER DIRECTIVE

Since publishing our proposed groundwater directive for notice and comment on May 6, 2014, we have heard from a number of states and other parties concerns about the intent of and language in the proposal. By the end of the comment period, we had received 260 unique comment submittals from elected officials, states, tribes, organizations, and individuals from across the country. This committee, as well as several states, asked us to not proceed with the proposed draft and to consult with them before moving forward. We have listened and are actively having those conversations now. We will continue to work cooperatively with this committee and the states and will not move forward until we can address the concerns raised. In fact, in recent hearings the Chief of the Forest Service stated that the proposed directive has been put on hold. We will publish a new draft for a new round of public comment before any direction is finalized. It is the intent of the Forest Service that nothing in the implementation of our stewardship responsibilities for National Forests and Grasslands infringes on state authority for water allocation and state and tribal authority for water quality protection.

The proposed directive on groundwater is intended to help the Agency establish a more consistent approach to evaluating and monitoring the effects on groundwater from actions on National Forest System (NFS) lands.

The proposed directive did not specifically authorize or prohibit any uses and did not represent an expansion of authority. The Forest Service recognized and specifically acknowledged in the proposed directives, the role of states in the allocation of water use and protection of water quality. The proposed directive would not and was not intended to infringe in any way on state authority, nor would it impose requirements on private landowners or change the long-standing relationship between the Forest Service and states and tribes on water.

Rather, it proposed a framework that would allow the Forest Service to clarify existing policy and better meet existing requirements in a more consistent way across NFS lands. Specifically, it was intended to:

- Improve our understanding of groundwater systems that influence and are influenced by surface uses on NFS land by creating a more consistent approach for gathering information;
- Support management and authorization of various multiple uses by creating a more consistent approach to evaluating, disclosing and monitoring the potential effects on groundwater resources of proposed activities on and uses of NFS lands in a way that supports informed and legally defensible decisions;
- Provide transparent and consistent direction for evaluating proposed Forest Service activities affecting groundwater resources on NFS lands and for quantifying the nature and extent of large groundwater withdrawals; and

- Emphasize cooperation with state, tribal and local agencies, recognizing all existing roles and responsibilities.

In many instances, the Forest Service has a legal obligation to analyze and disclose the impacts that activities it authorizes, funds, or undertakes directly may have on natural resources, including groundwater. In a number of examples around the country, multiple use decisions made by the Agency have been challenged in court, with plaintiffs arguing that such impacts were not fully analyzed or disclosed. This responsibility stems from direction in the Forest Service's Organic Act of 1897 (directing the Forest Service to manage NFS lands to secure favorable conditions of water flow); the Weeks Act of 1911 (for navigable stream protection); the Bankhead-Jones Act of 1935 (to mitigate floods, conserve surface and subsurface moisture, and protect watersheds); and the Multiple-Use Sustained-Yield Act of 1960, the National Forest Management Act of 1976, and the Federal Land Policy and Management Act of 1976 (all providing direction to the Forest Service regarding water, watersheds, and the management of natural resources including water).

Water on NFS lands is important for many reasons, including resource stewardship, domestic use, and public recreation. Today, water from national forests and grasslands contributes to the economic and ecological vitality of rural and urban communities across the Nation, and those lands supply more than 60 million Americans with clean drinking water.[1]

This role is increasingly important as drought conditions worsen in many parts of the country. On Wednesday, April 1, 2015, Governor Jerry Brown issued an executive order announcing a mandatory 25 percent reduction in water consumption in cities and towns across the state, following his previous declarations in January and April of 2014 of a state of emergency throughout California due to severe and ongoing drought conditions. Other parts of the country also face drought conditions: for example, 13 counties in Oregon and 11 counties in Washington State have received drought emergency declarations. Persistence and intensification of drought conditions is anticipated across the West.

NFS lands provide 18 percent of the Nation's freshwater and over half the freshwater in the West.[2] Groundwater plays a critical role in providing that freshwater, serving as a reservoir supplying cold, clean water to springs, streams, and wetlands, as well as water for human uses. Activities on national forests and grasslands can impact surface water, drinking water source areas, and groundwater reserves, including major aquifers (U.S. Geological Survey Principal Aquifers).

Through this proposed directive, the Forest Service would be better positioned to respond to changing conditions, such as drought, climate change, land use changes and needs for additional water supplies, in an informed manner, while sustaining the health and productivity of NFS lands and meeting new societal demands for resources in a responsible way. Our goal is to improve the quality and consistency of our approach to understanding groundwater resources on NFS lands and to better incorporate consideration of those resources to inform agency decisionmaking. Establishing a consistent framework for evaluating groundwater resources will also help to ensure that the Forest Service's decisions are well informed and can withstand legal challenge.

By improving the agency's ability to understand groundwater resources and have a more consistent, informed and legally defensible approach to evaluate, make decisions about, and monitor activities on NFS lands that could impact groundwater resources, the proposed directive would make the agency a better and more consistent partner to states, tribes, and project proponents, as well as to the downstream communities that depend on NFS lands for their drinking water. We look forward to continuing the productive conversations we are currently having with the committee, states, and other partners, as well as to receiving additional feedback through another formal comment period.

This concludes my testimony and I would be happy to answer any questions.

---

[1] http://www.fs.fed.us/publications/policy-analysis/water.pdf.

[2] www.fs.fed.us/pnw/pubs/pnw_gtr812.pdf.

QUESTIONS SUBMITTED FOR THE RECORD BY THE HON. DAN NEWHOUSE TO
DEPUTY CHIEF LESLIE WELDON, U.S. FOREST SERVICE

Ms. Weldon did not submit responses to the Committee by the appropriate deadline for inclusion in the printed record.

Question 1. Recently, I have heard a lot of complaints about the Forest Service and the manner in which the Service has been interacting with communities in central Washington. I am very concerned with the lack of communication and the inability of the Service to hold forums and take comments on rulemakings and proposals without offending local constituencies. From the proposal to introduce grizzlies in the North Cascades and the proposed "groundwater directive," to the Okanogan-Wenatchee National Forest Travel Management Plan and NW Forest Management Plan—I have heard numerous complaints that people feel their voices are not being heard and that the Service is not taking local concerns into consideration. One of my constituents from Kennewick recently sent a letter to the Forest Service and I would like to read this excerpt that really sums up these concerns:

> *"What happened to the Forest Service my Aunt, Father-in-Law, and I worked for? You know, the one where the Forest Service was part of the community and took part in the life of the community. It seems like too many of your folks don't stay anywhere long enough to get any kind of feel for what works on any given forest. It's time the FS got back to basics, and started acting like who you are, stewards, not owners. Where is the economic interest of so many communities being considered? It really isn't. Rural communities that rely on the forests for resources and commodity production are suffering under the current regime."*

I was pleased to hear that the Service corrected course and will now be holding additional listening sessions on the local forest plan revision. In that vein, can you tell me what measures are currently being undertaken to improve the way your agency interacts with local communities? Are there any efforts underway to improve your coordination with local stakeholders and to better incorporate their needs and concerns?

Question 2. One of our witnesses stated that the language of the Groundwater Directive "misleadingly suggests that the U.S. Forest Service has equal authority with the state over groundwater management". Despite the fact that the Directive has been withdrawn, does the Forest Service believe that states have primacy over groundwater management?

Question 3. As it relates to groundwater litigation, most of the examples you provided the committee were mining examples where BLM has responsibility for analyzing the activity. Does BLM analyze sub-surface impacts? Are they not doing their job?

Question 4. Deputy Chief Weldon, you mentioned that you intend to coordinate with states and others. After you talk with the states and other Federal agencies, if the majority of the states are still not supportive of this Directive or a future Forest Service groundwater policy, do you still intend to move forward with the Groundwater Directive or a similarly focused policy?

––––––––––

Dr. FLEMING. Thank you, Ms. Weldon. I now recognize myself for 5 minutes for questions.

One of our witnesses stated that the language of the Groundwater Directive "misleadingly suggests that the U.S. Forest Service has equal authority with the state over groundwater management." Does the Forest Service believe that the states have primacy over groundwater management?

Ms. WELDON. The work that we are doing now to respond to concerns is one that really has us digging in to understanding the authorities of the states. And we agree that the states do have that lead role in making determination on water quality and water availability. So we feel like we need to coordinate very closely with them on our goal of being able to ensure that we are assessing correctly the resource impacts for any activities that are proposed on national forest land that may affect groundwater.

Dr. FLEMING. Would "lead role" be the same as primacy?

Ms. WELDON. I am not a lawyer, so I wouldn't want to—but we definitely acknowledge that the states carry that lead role in making those determinations on availability.

Dr. FLEMING. As it relates to groundwater litigation, most of the examples you provided the committee were mining examples, where BLM has responsibility for analyzing the activity. Does BLM analyze subsurface impacts?

Ms. WELDON. BLM is predominantly responsible for analyzing subsurface impacts for minerals and for water use.

Dr. FLEMING. OK. Are they not doing their job in this?

Ms. WELDON. We work very closely and cooperatively with BLM. But this directive is really about our ability to make sure we are providing consistent, clear direction across our whole system. So, our goal with the directive was to put that in place, which I think will enable us to work more strongly with the BLM, and with the states.

Dr. FLEMING. You indicated that you do not intend to go forward on a revised groundwater directive. Does that mean you are not coming up with a groundwater directive in the next year-and-a-half?

Ms. WELDON. We haven't set a time frame. But at this point we have stopped with the current proposal, and we won't move forward with another one until we have done the job of that close collaboration and co-development with the states, so that, when we get to that point—and I don't have a date for it—of issuing a new proposal for that internal guidance, it will be one that comes with that strong support, and we will be sure to coordinate with Congress as we get to that point.

Dr. FLEMING. What was the reason for standing down on moving forward with the directive? What was the main purpose of that, or the reason why you chose not to go forward?

Ms. WELDON. What we found in the response to our comments, and from the concerns expressed by the states, by tribes, and others, that we needed to do a much stronger job of ensuring that our intent with this directive for guidance was one that wasn't seen as compromising our relationships or ability for the states to do their jobs.

So, we will have a stronger directive and proposal eventually, based on us pausing, having this level of coordination, that we can take this to a better place.

Dr. FLEMING. You said you intended to coordinate with states and others after you talk with the states and other Federal agencies. If a majority of states are still not supportive, do you still intend to move forward with the policy?

I hear again you are saying, "Well, the states should lead," which, to me, to my ears, doesn't sound like primacy, necessarily. So there may be a distinction without a difference, maybe not. And so you are saying we, the Federal Government, should work cooperatively with the state governments. But what if you come to an impasse, and they are not on board with what you want to do? What happens then?

Ms. WELDON. Well, we hope that we can come to as much clarity as possible. And that may mean that different states will have different requirements for implementing, or eventually moving forward, with a rule. We want to leave the space for those determinations to be made. But I can't predict, ultimately, how we would resolve those, until we get further into the process.

Dr. FLEMING. OK. I yield to the Ranking Member, Mr. Huffman.

Mr. HUFFMAN. Thank you, Mr. Chairman. I just want to comment about this empty chair theater regarding the Bureau of Reclamation that has sort of been playing out as part of the hearing.

It is true that the Bureau of Reclamation, which has no authority or jurisdiction involving the Clean Water Act, which was the stated purpose of this hearing, is not here. Neither is the Department of Defense, the Department of Homeland Security, NASA, or the Veterans Administration. They are not here, either. And all of those agencies have about as much relevance to the subject of the Clean Water Act as any of the others. The Bureau never agreed to be here. The Bureau is not required to be here. And the absence of the Bureau, frankly, in no way detracts from whatever legitimacy this hearing might have, which is not much.

I did want to speak, though, to the comments from my colleague, Mr. McClintock, in apparently correcting me about state preemption in the Valadao bill. Fortunately, he and others don't have to take my word for it—the state of California itself took a position that the bill would have been preemptive, including the state Attorney General, whose job it is to defend California water law. So I am happy to correct the correction on that point.

And Ms. Weldon, turning to you, thank you for doing what the record clearly shows you did. You listened, you had a deliberative, inclusive process that had outreach, and you took comments, concerns, and you are now moving forward in a very collaborative, thoughtful way. I don't think you are going to get a lot of thank-you notes from the Majority in this committee for being inclusive and thoughtful. Around here, no good deed goes unpunished. But I think it is obvious that the Forest Service is listening, and trying to get this right. And there is really nothing more that we can ask of you than that.

Now, if we were to have an oversight hearing involving the Forest Service and water on a subject that is of relevance, that is ripe and important right now, it might involve the fact that, in California, where we are experiencing a critical drought, heading into the fourth year of a drought, the Forest Service has allowed Nestle Waters of North America to continue using a pipeline to transport spring water out of the San Bernardino National Forest on a permit that expired almost three decades ago. It has not conducted any scientific assessment of Nestle's use of the water from those springs, how it could be impacting wildlife and groundwater.

So, we might very well, if we were interested in problems involving the Forest Service and water management that are relevant, be asking whether the Forest Service is doing enough to protect California's scarce water resources from a company like Nestle, operating without a permit right now in this critical drought environment.

I am going to give you an opportunity to speak to that, if you like. It is certainly a subject I would like to take up with you separately. But while we had you here, I thought I would at least raise the question.

Ms. WELDON. And thank you for your question. We would be happy to meet with you to go into detail about our approach forward with the special use permit for Nestle, for their accessing water.

I will share that the California region in the San Bernardino National Forest have seen the need now, and are actively pursuing their next steps, as far as evaluating this permit, looking to what is going to be necessary to evaluate the current work that is happening with accessing water. And we will be happy to share with you the next steps out of that, as it relates to resolving this permit that has gone so long without being renewed.

Mr. HUFFMAN. All right. I appreciate that. Thanks for your testimony. I yield back.

Dr. FLEMING. Before I recognize the next gentleman, I want to clarify for our committee, this committee does have jurisdiction over the Department of Reclamation. And issues are relevant to them, and we did ask them. We don't have jurisdiction over DoD. They don't have relevance to this, and we didn't ask them to come. So I want to be sure everybody understands that.

With that, I will recognize Dr. Gosar.

Dr. GOSAR. Thank you, Mr. Chairman. And thank you, Ms. Weldon, for showing up. We certainly appreciate it. And thanks for the revocation of the groundwater rule. We appreciate that aspect.

I want to touch on another aspect, because I want to talk about the Federal Government moving again in ski area jurisdictional aspects. So I have a couple statements here.

The latest Forest Service ski area clauses are the fourth different proposal in 10 years on this matter. You all continue to come out with significantly flawed initiatives that receive considerable backlash from local stakeholders and Members of Congress in both parties. Then you revise these proposals to see what you can get away with. But I am convinced you just don't get it.

The Western Governors' Association Executive Director testified today and expressed serious concern about the latest ski area clauses, stating—and I quote—''Certain terms within the proposed initiative are undefined, creating ambiguity for states and permittees. For instance, the clause requires water rights holders to obtain advance written approval from the U.S. Forest Service before water rights can be divided, transferred, or modified if such action will adversely affect the availability of those rights to support operation of the ski area.'' End of quote.

Advance written approval from the Forest Service for water rights that the ski areas have invested hundreds of millions of dollars on to support their operations. Right? That is—in many cases, they have invested all this money for this infrastructure aspect, right? Sounds like more bureaucracy and red tape, to me.

Who are the perceived bad actors in this issue?

Ms. WELDON. I thank you for your question. And what I believe our intent is, or what our intent is, indeed, is to ensure that, as we are looking at continuing to provide this recreational opportunity that is based on national forest land, that, as we look at transferring permits, or any other changes, that there is water available.

So, we are working very closely right now, through the clauses that you have——

Dr. GOSAR. Yes, but you don't—you, as a Federal agency, don't have jurisdiction over that water. That is states rights. Is it not?

Ms. WELDON. We agree, absolutely, that——

Dr. GOSAR. That is my whole point here, is the overreach of that aspect. I mean in rural Arizona, particularly, like, in Flagstaff, I mean, when you are considering groundwater, which also serves Flagstaff, but also the community up on the ski area up there, you are talking about 80 percent of that groundwater being utilized in this instance. So there is a reason why people—like, Flagstaff in Arizona, which rely on a lot of groundwater—are up in arms about this. Because you don't need your hands on it.

Now, can you name me one instance a ski area that sold off its water rights?

Ms. WELDON. No, I cannot.

Dr. GOSAR. It has never happened. In fact, even your boss, Forest Service Tom Tidwell, said as much in his testimony before this committee. It seems to me that the latest ski area clause is really just another proposed water grab of a different problem. Do you agree?

Ms. WELDON. I do not agree. Our goal is to ensure that, if we are going to provide——

Dr. GOSAR. Once again, let's go back——

Ms. WELDON [continuing]. National forest land, there needs to be water——

Dr. GOSAR. I don't want to interrupt you, but who has primacy on that subsurface water?

Ms. WELDON. That is the state.

Dr. GOSAR. So what are you messing with, in this aspect? I mean, from that standpoint, that is part of the problem here, is the states have done a pretty darn good job.

I mean, in Arizona we have this mantra, "whiskey is for drinking, water is for fighting over." And it is true, because we should have probably served whiskey up here, because we are going to be in a hurting aspect. We are not probably going to be as bad as California. I don't want to get between you and Mr. McClintock, though.

Ms. WELDON. We are running out of states, too, for——

Dr. GOSAR. Yes, but that is my point, that in defining water law, the subsurface water is that of the states. And hands need to be off from the Federal Government. And I think, from that standpoint, let's not go back here and create more dissatisfaction—I can't even speak any more today. That is what happens when you get between two Californians.

Ms. WELDON. I——

Dr. GOSAR. My point is it ought to come off the table. Because that application is about extortion. You are extorting water rights that are primacy of the states. And I would hope that you would remove that. Otherwise, be prepared for taking more barrage from communities like this, Flagstaff, Arizona, other states—Colorado is another one. So just my words of warning.

Ms. WELDON. OK, thank you.

Dr. GOSAR. Like I said, whiskey is for drinking, water is for fighting over.

Thanks, Ms. Weldon.

Ms. WELDON. Yes, thanks.

Dr. FLEMING. OK. Well, we thank you, Deputy Weldon, for your valuable testimony.

Ms. WELDON. Thank you.

Dr. FLEMING. Members of the subcommittee may have additional questions for you, as our witness, and we ask that you respond in writing.

And, there being no further business today, without objection, this subcommittee stands adjourned.

[Whereupon, at 3:53 p.m., the subcommittee was adjourned.]

[ADDITIONAL MATERIALS SUBMITTED FOR THE RECORD]

PREPARED STATEMENT OF THE BUREAU OF RECLAMATION, U.S. DEPARTMENT OF THE INTERIOR

The Bureau of Reclamation (Reclamation) submits the following statement in response to the subcommittee's hearing titled "Proposed Federal Water Grabs and their Potential Impacts on States, Water and Power Users, and Landowners." This statement builds on last year's statement to this subcommittee for the June 24, 2014 hearing titled, "New Federal Schemes to Soak Up Water Authority: Impacts on States, Water Users, Recreation and Jobs", which was focused on the same proposed rulemaking.

As noted in last year's statement, we recognize the subcommittee's interest in assuring that Federal regulations do not adversely impact our environment and economy, and we appreciate the desire for a clear understanding of the 2014 proposed rule regarding the definition of "Waters of the United States" under the Clean Water Act (Act). As this subcommittee is aware, the proposed rule was issued by the Environmental Protection Agency (EPA) and Army Corps of Engineers (Corps) who have jurisdiction over the Clean Water Act. Reclamation has outlined its views on the proposed rule below; however, Reclamation does not have jurisdictional authority in interpreting the Clean Water Act nor implementing regulations thereunder. We believe that EPA and the Corps are the appropriate entities to discuss the details of their proposed rule, as they did in depth in a joint hearing before the Senate Committee on Environment and Public Works and House Committee on Transportation and Infrastructure on February 4, 2015.

On April 21, 2014, the Federal Register published the proposed rule from the EPA and Corps [1] that is the subject of today's hearing. Titled the "Definition of 'Waters of the United States' Under the Clean Water Act," the proposed rule was published in response to longstanding uncertainty about the scope of waters regulated under the Act. As stated in the materials accompanying the proposed rule's release, Members of Congress, state and local officials, industry, agriculture, environmental groups, and the public have asked for nearly a decade that a rulemaking occur to provide clarity on the scope of Federal jurisdiction under the Act.

Since that time, interested congressional committees including those with jurisdiction over EPA and the Corps have held several hearings and Members have introduced at least three pieces of legislation or amendments to other bills, specifically targeting the proposed rule. Early this year, EPA and the Corps withdrew the interpretive rule which aimed to clarify the existing 404(f)(1)(A) exemption under the Clean Water Act in compliance with specific congressional direction to withdraw the interpretive rule, contained in Section 112 of the FY 2015 Consolidated Appropriation (P.L. 113–235).

While we continue to believe that EPA and the Corps are the appropriate entities to discuss the details of their proposed rule, it remains our understanding that the

---

[1] http://www2.epa.gov/sites/production/files/2014-04/documents/fr-2014-07142.pdf.

proposed rule was never designed to expand the Act's applicability beyond existing regulation; that it is not designed to cover groundwater; and that the rule does not expand the Act's reach to cover additional irrigation ditches or alter the existing water transfers exclusion, which are obviously of special relevance for Reclamation. For the purposes of Reclamation's water and power mission areas that are of interest to this subcommittee, Reclamation shares the interest of our stakeholders in preserving our shared ability to operate and maintain facilities and deliver water and power. To that end, we were pleased that EPA and the Corps have included a proposed exclusion in the rule for ditches excavated wholly in uplands and draining only uplands, with less than perennial flow, including those that may carry groundwater. The significance of this detail is that ditches excavated for drainage purposes in uplands on agricultural lands are unlikely to serve their intended function unless they carry flow at least intermittently, so it is important that ditches with intermittent flow be eligible for the proposed exclusion.

We are encouraged that the EPA and Corps worked with state and tribal partners to assure these voices are effectively represented during this rulemaking process. We appreciate EPA and the Corps' efforts to improve clarity and preserve existing Clean Water Act exemptions and exclusions for agriculture. For example, we appreciate that the rule does not change, in any way, existing Clean Water Act exemptions from permitting under Section 404 for discharges of dredged and/or fill material in waters of the U.S. associated with normal farming, silviculture, and ranching activities, such as upland soil and water conservation practices; construction and maintenance of farm or stock ponds or irrigation ditches, or the maintenance of drainage ditches; and construction or maintenance of farm, forest, and temporary mining roads, where constructed and maintained in accordance with best management practices. We also appreciate that the rule does not change, in any way, existing Clean Water Act exemptions from permitting for agricultural stormwater discharges and return flows from irrigated agriculture.

The EPA and the Corps extended the public comment period on the proposed rule twice until November 14, 2014 in order to provide a full and effective opportunity for public comment. The public docket shows that over one million public comments on the proposed rule have been gathered by the agencies, and as part of the rulemaking process the EPA and the Corps would review the comments received by all entities, including comments submitted by participants in today's hearing, as they prepare revisions that provide additional clarity regarding the geographical scope of the Clean Water Act.

The Clean Water Act is over four decades old, with several instances of litigation over Congress's true intentions in passing the law, and we recognize the value in updated regulations to guide its implementation. Reclamation shares the interest of our stakeholders in preserving our shared ability to operate and maintain facilities and deliver water and power. As with the proposed rule, Reclamation will continue to participate in the interagency review process in support of our collective interests, as the agencies work to finalize or revise the rule consistent with congressional direction.

Thank you for the opportunity to participate in today's hearing.

———

CALIFORNIA ASSOCIATION OF SANITATION AGENCIES,
SACRAMENTO, CA,
NOVEMBER 5, 2014.

Water Docket, Environmental Protection Agency, Mail Code 2822T
1200 Pennsylvania Avenue NW
Washington, DC 20460
Attention: Docket ID No. EPA–HQ–OW–2011–0880

Re: Comments of the California Association of Sanitation Agencies on the Proposed Rule Defining ''Waters of the United States''

Dear Administrator McCarthy:

The California Association of Sanitation Agencies (CASA) is pleased to provide comments on the proposed rule to define ''Waters of the United States'' (hereafter ''proposed rule'') under the federal Clean Water Act (CWA). CASA represents more than 100 local public wastewater agencies engaged in collecting, treating and recycling wastewater to ensure protection of public health and the environment. Collectively, our agencies serve over 90 percent of the sewered population of California. CASA's member agencies operate wastewater treatment and water recycling facilities that discharge into waters of the United States as well as to waters of the state, and as such they may be impacted by the proposed rule's promulgation as well as its implementation.

CASA appreciates that the proposed rule explicitly specifies that the agencies propose no changes to the longstanding regulations that exclude waste treatment systems designed to meet the requirements of the CWA and prior converted cropland from the definition of "Waters of the United States." (79 FR 22217) These regulations provide an essential component of the existing regulatory framework that ensures effective agency operations. The retention of the waste treatment exemption is one of the highest priorities for clean water agencies. We also endorse the proposed rule's clarification that the agencies do not intend alter the regulation of groundwater at the federal level and, in fact, the proposed rule codifies a number of the waters and features that the agencies have by longstanding practice generally considered not to be "Waters of the United States." (*Id.* at 22218)

CASA holds several concerns about the expansion of federal jurisdiction under the proposed rule and potentially adverse ramifications for wastewater agencies across the state and the Nation. Our primary concerns are: (1) the lack of clarity in the proposed rule as to what is included in the waste treatment exemption will create regulatory barriers to the effective implementation of recycled water projects without a commensurate benefit to the environment, thereby threatening recycled water projects that are vital to California water supply; and (2) expansion of jurisdictional waters under the proposed rule that could complicate and interfere with aspects of the wastewater treatment process. Specific issues and the manner in which the proposed rule could impact wastewater agencies are provided in more detail below.

The Waste Treatment Exemption Should Specifically Include Water Recycling Facilities and Effluent Storage Ponds

In order to address the historic drought conditions currently plaguing the western states, water and wastewater agencies must rely on a full suite of flexible options to provide potable and recycled water supplies for a variety of ongoing uses. Thus, CASA opposes any direct or indirect regulatory impacts on water recycling, water storage, and other mechanisms that playa part in recycled water infrastructure and processes as a result of the proposed rule.

As noted above, we appreciate the explicit acknowledgement and codification of the waste treatment exemption in the proposed rule. However, we believe it is important that the proposed rule **expressly** states that the waste treatment exemption extends to recycled water facilities. California water recycling projects often depend upon artificially created wetlands and storage ponds to treat millions of gallons of water a day. If these features are considered waters of the U.S. and are excluded from the waste treatment exemption, they could theoretically no longer be used as an integral component of the waste treatment systems, forcing the closure of important recycled water projects critical to California's water supply. Moreover, a lack of clarity on this issue may stall or halt the development of recycled water projects at a time when recycling is needed the most to address climate resiliency priorities.

Because recycled water demand is variable with time of day and season, recycled water agencies maintain reservoirs or store basins/ponds to store recycled water during periods of low usage in anticipation of peak demands. These features are an essential component of the recycled water process and integral to an agency's ability to continue reliably producing and supplying recycled water in many instances. The proposed rule should affirm that such reservoirs along with influent and treated effluent storage ponds are within the scope of the waste treatment exemption, consistent with the regulatory definition of "complete waste treatment system" found in existing federal regulations.[1] As the proposed rule and existing practice acknowledge, waste treatment systems designed to meet the requirements of the Clean Water Act are not waters of the U.S., and treatment systems should include any

---

[1] See 40 C.F.R. §35.2005(b)(12), defining "complete waste treatment system" as "all the treatment works necessary to meet the requirements of title III of the [CWA], involving . . . the ultimate disposal, *including recycling or reuse*, of the treated wastewater and residues which result from the treatment process." (Emphasis added); *see also* 40 C.F.R. §35.2005(b)(49) [definition of "treatment works" includes "storage of treated wastewater in land treatment systems before land application" among other things]

facilities, including storage ponds and basins, related not only to traditional treatment facilities and processes, but also to the production of recycled water.

In the alternative, recycled water facilities and features (including storage ponds, basins, artificially created wetlands, recycled water reservoirs and other features associated with water recycling) should be expressly exempted as part of the specifically identified features that are not considered waters of the U.S. within the proposed rule. In this case, recycled water facilities would be treated similar to artificial lakes, ponds, swimming pools, ornamental waters, and groundwater, which are specifically identified and expressly exempted. In either case, whether recycled water facilities are considered part of the waste treatment exemption or have their own specifically identified exemption, it is essential that the proposed rule not interfere with recycled water production and treatment by making those features jurisdictional.

The failure to include an explicit statement in the final rule would leave open the question of whether these features are considered "Waters of the U.S." Such a situation could lead to regulatory disincentives to produce recycled water in California and other western states, compounding a water scarcity situation that is already dire. Pending and adopted federal and state legislation to address the impacts of our historic drought contain a number of approaches to encourage recycled water projects. Transforming components of the recycled water process (including integral systems such as storage ponds) into jurisdictional waters would completely undercut efforts to address the drought and have resoundingly negative water supply ramifications across the state. We concur with the comments of Representative Grace Napolitano (D-CA) delivered to the House Committee on Transportation and Infrastructure Committee at the hearing held on June 11, 2014, as she questioned why in light of the severe drought in California, USEPA would not expressly include recycled water within the scope of the waste treatment exception. Given the drought and dire need to develop recycled water facilities in the arid west, clarification that excludes recycled water facilities from additional federal regulation is absolutely vital.

Spreading Grounds and Related Features of the Wastewater Treatment Process Should Be Expressly Exempted Under the Final Rule

As the proposed rule and existing practice acknowledge, waste treatment systems designed to meet the requirements of the Clean Water Act are not waters of the U.S., and CASA wants to ensure that as part of these proposed amendments spreading grounds/basins, treatment ponds/lagoons, and constructed treatment wetlands used as part of the wastewater process are subject to the same exemption. Since these facilities are clearly part of the treatment process, providing additional treatment, residence and settling prior to discharge, these facilities should be expressly recognized in the rule as falling under the Waste Treatment Exception.

In addition, many CASA member agencies utilize spreading grounds or basins in order to facilitate groundwater replenishment; a vital part of water management throughout California. Others utilize artificially created effluent storage ponds as part of their treatment process. Many agencies maintain reservoirs or storage basins/ponds to store recycled water. These artificially created features and spreading grounds have not previously been defined or regulated as "Waters of the United States," and should remain separate. For this reason, the proposed rule should expressly include treatment ponds/lagoons, spreading grounds/basins, and constructed treatment wetlands within the scope of the Waste Treatment Exception, along with effluent storage reservoirs and recycled water storage facilities discussed previously.

The Proposed Amendments to What is Considered an "Adjacent Water" Must be Reexamined to Consider Wastewater Treatment Processes

Many wastewater treatment processes, including man-made spreading basins, are located near or even "adjacent" to rivers and tributaries that have been (or under the proposed rule, would be) designated as waters of the U.S. and may be located in the riparian or floodplain areas of these rivers. Because the proposed rule defines "adjacency" and includes the incorporation of waters within the flood plain or riparian area of a designated water of the U.S. as also being a jurisdictional water (see section 328.3(c)(2)–(4), FR 22263), this could lead to an interpretation that such spreading basins and artificial storage ponds are jurisdictional.

Specifically, the proposed rule would revise the current category of an "adjacent wetland" to include all "adjacent waters." (FR 22206) As a result, numerous treatment ponds, recycled water reservoirs, and spreading grounds/basins across California could become jurisdictional, creating a significant problem and interference with existing wastewater treatment processes. For example, under the proposed rule, the Montebello Forebay spreading grounds in southern California would appear to become jurisdictional. Under existing rules, regulations and case law, a waterbody is considered a water of the U.S. if it is wetland adjacent to a water of the U.S. In contrast, under the proposed rule, all waterbodies (of many types) adjacent to a water of the U.S. could be considered themselves waters of the U.S., regardless of whether any sort of nexus or hydraulic connection has been shown and without any consideration of whether a berm or levee separates them. Under the proposed rule, a significant nexus appears to be assumed, as it states ". . . even in cases where a hydrologic connection may not exist, there are other important considerations . . . that result in a significant nexus between the adjacent wetlands or waters and the nearby "Waters of the United States" and (a)(1) through (a)(3) waters." (79 FR 22244) As one seeming justification for this expanded interpretation, the proposed rule states that "many major species that prefer habitats at the interface of wetland and stream ecosystems remain able to utilize both habitats despite the presence of such a berm." (*Id.* at 22245) This use of species preference and behavior to justify incorporation of a water with no proven hydrologic connection as a water of the U.S. closely resembles the previously invalidated migratory bird rule. As such, terrestrial species preference is not an acceptable basis for the assertion of jurisdiction.

If these "adjacent" wastewater and recycled water facilities, including spreading grounds, are defined to be within the jurisdiction of the CWA, it would adversely impact CASA's member agencies' ability to augment groundwater supplies and to effectively provide wastewater treatment services. The plethora of additional and unnecessary requirements, regulations, and permitting associated with making these areas into jurisdictional waters, including but not limited to the procurement of an NPDES permit, assigning designated uses, exposure to penalties and potential third party liability for effluent violations, and impairment of the ability to operate and maintain these areas, would erect new mandates with no benefit to the surrounding ecosystems and waterbodies. Such a result represents an extreme disincentive to sustainable water supply development and a significant impairment of wastewater agencies' ability to protect public health and safety through innovative and effective wastewater treatment.

Within the proposed rule, there are two specific exemptions that could potentially address this issue. Pursuant to section 328.3(b)(5)(i) and 122.2(b)(5)(i),[2] a spreading ground could fall under the definition of "[a]rtificially irrigated areas that would revert to upland should application of irrigation water to that area cease" (79 FR 22263 and 22268) Spreading grounds utilized by wastewater treatment facilities are generally artificially created and might not otherwise exist aside from the application of wastewater effluent to the area. However, without being explicitly stated, it is not clear enough that this definition would apply to upland wastewater spreading grounds. Similarly, pursuant to section 328.3(b)(5)(ii) and 122.2(b)(5)(ii), wastewater and recycled water ponds and spreading grounds could fall under an expanded definition of "[a]rtificial lakes or ponds created by excavating and/or diking dry land and used exclusively for such purposes as stock water, irrigation, settling basins, or rice growing." (79 FR 22263 and 22268) The word "such" seems to indicate that these are merely examples, not an exhaustive list, and thus spreading grounds utilized in conjunction with and/or as part of the overall wastewater treatment process could fall under this exclusion. However, without specific references within these provisions to treatment ponds and spreading grounds, CASA and its members are very concerned that these facilities could become jurisdictional and create significant problems for agencies attempting to protect public health and the environment. This, we would request the explicit inclusion of the terms such as "spreading grounds" and "wastewater and recycled water storage," within this section.

"Tributary" is Defined Too Broadly and Will Likely be Construed to Include Certain Conveyances and Ditches

For the first time, the proposed rule seeks to define what constitutes a "tributary" under the Clean Water Act. The proposed rule drastically expands the number of waters potentially subject to federal jurisdiction. Specifically, the proposed rule defines "tributary" as a water "physically characterized by the presence of a bed and banks and ordinary high water mark . . . which contributes flow, either directly or through another water . . ." to a water of the U.S. (79 FR 22201–22202) Even wet-

---

[2] All references are to Part 328 and Part 122, however the language suggestions contained herein similarly apply to other regulatory sections that have the potential to impact wastewater entities, including Part 230 (79 FR 22268–22269), Part 232 (79 FR 22269–22270), and Part 401 (79 FR 22273–22274).

lands, lakes, and ponds without an ordinary high water mark (OHWM) or bed and banks would be considered tributaries if they contribute flow, either directly or through another water to a water of the U.S. (*Id.* at 22201–22202) Perhaps most significantly, under the proposed rule, a tributary, including wetlands, can be a natural, man-altered, or man-made water and includes waters such as rivers, streams, lakes, ponds, impoundments, canals, and ditches not otherwise explicitly excluded. (*Id.* at 22202)

This overly broad definition of tributary could potentially increase the number of man-made conveyances, ditches and conveyance facilities, including those utilized by wastewater entities, under federal jurisdiction, and the lack of certainty surrounding the rule's definition of a tributary could lead to regulation of previously unregulated waters. This broad classification of "tributaries" would be considered jurisdictional regardless of perennial, intermittent or ephemeral flow. Even dry washes could be considered jurisdictional under the proposed rule. This is significant for a variety of reasons.

One example of the potential impacts of defining what constitutes a "tributary" too broadly is the potential discharge from sanitary sewer systems to dry creeks/sloughs/washes when no pollutants ever actually reach water. It is entirely unclear whether this constitutes a discharge of pollutants to a water of the U.S. Under the broad definition of tributary in the proposed rule, it is possible that spills to dry creeks, sloughs, or washes would be considered a "discharge" even if there is absolutely no real or potential impacts to surface waters of any kind. Similarly, there are circumstances where sewer spills occur in a street that drains to a roadside ditch or local creek bed that has no flow and is unconnected to a water of the U.S. The responsible party may fully remediate the spill and address all real and potential water quality impacts before the spill ever reaches a water source. It is difficult to understand how can this kind of circumstance could be envisioned as a discharge to "Waters of the United States" when there is no actual water in a dry creek or ditch nor an adverse impact to the environment.

CASA appreciates your consideration of our comments. If you have questions or wish to discuss our perspective further, please contact Adam D. Link, CASA's Director of Government Affairs at (916) 446–0388 or Eric Sapirstein, CASA's federal representative, at (202) 466–3755. Thank you for your consideration of our comments.

    Sincerely,

ADAM D. LINK,
CASA Director of Government Affairs.

––––––

CALIFORNIA WATER BOARDS,
STATE WATER RESOURCES CONTROL BOARD,
SACRAMENTO, CA,
NOVEMBER 14, 2014.

Hon. GINA MCCARTHY, *Administrator,*
Environmental Protection Agency,
1200 Pennsylvania Avenue NW (4101M),
Washington, DC 20460.

Hon. JO-ELLEN DARCY, *Assistant Secretary of the Army,*
Department of the Army,
108 Army Pentagon, Room 3E446,
Washington, DC 22310–0108.

Re: WATERS OF THE UNITED STATES PROPOSED RULE DOCKET ID NO. EPA–HQ–OW–2011–0880

Dear Administrator McCarthy and Assistant Secretary Darcy:

Thank you for the opportunity to comment on the U.S. Environmental Protection Agency and U.S. Department of the Army's (collectively the "Agencies") jointly

Proposed Rule,[1] which defines the scope of "Waters of the United States" protected under the federal Clean Water Act (CWA) in light of recent U.S. Supreme Court cases. The California State Water Resources Control Board (State Water Board), in conjunction with the nine California regional water quality control boards (collectively, "Water Boards"), is designated as California's water pollution control agency for the CWA. The Proposed Rule will affect all of the CWA programs that are administered by the Water Boards, including section 401 water quality certification, section 402 permitting, and section 303 water quality standards. Therefore, please accept the following general comments, as well as the attached specific comments, on the Proposed Rule on behalf of staff of the Water Boards.

We strongly support the Agencies' intent to adopt regulations to provide clarity to the definition of "Waters of the United States" in order to improve efficiency, consistency, and predictability while protecting water quality, public health, and the environment. Protection of water resources is of utmost importance in California. The availability of clean water, now and in the future, is vital to maintaining the health of our communities, businesses, agriculture, and natural environment, especially in the face of climate change and increased demand from a growing population. A comprehensive rulemaking represents a major improvement over the status quo, which is distinguished primarily by case-by-case jurisdictional determinations resulting in a patchwork of fact-specific, sometimes conflicting, judicial decisions. Neither the economy nor the environment is well served by the current regulatory uncertainty.

We also strongly support the Agencies' science-based approach to the rulemaking, particularly with respect to further defining the types of water bodies that are considered to be "Waters of the United States" because they significantly affect the chemical, physical, or biological integrity of traditional navigable waters, interstate waters, or the territorial seas.

For example, the inclusion of all tributaries (including headwaters, ephemeral and intermittent streams, and tributary wetlands and ponds) as jurisdictional waters is an important step in protecting water quality in California. Both the Agencies' peer-reviewed scientific report and the Science Advisory Board's October 17, 2014 review of the Agencies' report correctly recognize the importance of all tributaries in maintaining the biological, physical, and chemical integrity of downstream waters. As shown in Attachment A of this letter, intermittent and ephemeral streams cover a significant portion of California's surface area. As recommended by the Science Advisory Board in its September 30, 2014 letter to the Agencies, however, the Agencies should consider whether the proposed definition of "tributary" actually includes all ephemeral streams as intended, but also clearly distinguishes such tributaries from excluded non-tributary ditches. In addition, natural discontinuous channels in dry land stream systems should also be considered to be tributaries, even when there are one or more natural breaks in the channel.

Similarly, we support the proposed definition of "adjacent" waters as applying to all types of waters, not just wetlands. We also support the proposed definition of "neighboring" waters to include waters within "riparian" areas and "floodplains," as well as waters with a hydrologic connection to jurisdictional waters, because the science clearly indicates that these types of waters have a significant nexus to the jurisdictional waters.

These proposed new definitions of types of "Waters of the United States" offer increased clarity and consistency, which will result in more efficient and effective protection of headwaters, streams, their associated wetlands, and adjacent waters. This is important in states such as California that are characterized by a broad diversity of landscapes, climate, and hydrology. To the extent that the science justifies defining additional types of waters as "Waters of the United States," either now or in the future, we would support doing so for the same reasons. For example, as suggested by the Science Advisory Board in its September 30, 2014 letter to the Agencies, the Agencies should consider whether geographically based subcategories of similarly situated "other waters" have a significant nexus to jurisdictional waters. To the extent that is necessary to continue to rely instead on case-by-case significant nexus determinations, however, we generally support the framework of the Proposed Rule for similarly situated "other waters."

As recommended by the Scientific Advisory Board in its September 30, 2014 letter to the Agencies, the Agencies should also consider whether non-wetland swales and other features that provide hydrologic connectivity to and between wetland complexes, such as vernal pools, should be excluded if they directly contribute flows, and

[1] As published in 79 Fed. Reg. 22188–22274 (April 21, 2014)

function as part of the tributary system to jurisdictional waters, even though they lack an ordinary high water mark and bed and bank. Additionally, while we generally support the exclusion of ditches, gullies, and rills from "Waters of the United States," we recommend that these features be defined to avoid confusion. To the extent that any excluded features can contribute flow to waters of the United States, the Agencies should clarify that they may be considered point sources, as long as they are not statutorily exempt from regulation under the CWA.

Some states, including California, have state laws that supplement the CWA's authority to protect certain types of water bodies. Even so, we appreciate the necessity of relying on the authority provided by CWA section 401 to regulate discharges to waters of the United States, especially for discharges associated with projects licensed by the Federal Energy Regulatory Commission. A narrow definition of "Waters of the United States" would mean that state authority over more of these types of projects would be preempted by the Federal Power Act.

In a similar vein, we rely heavily on the Agencies' activities under the section 404 dredge and fill program to leverage our limited staff resources in the section 401 water quality certification program. A narrow definition of "Waters of the United States" would require additional state resources to achieve the same level of protection as is afforded under the section 404 program today. By contrast, the proposed definition of "Waters of the United States" will not increase the type and number of water bodies that are protected only under state law, and will also reduce the number of case-by-case determinations. This will facilitate the processing of CWA section 401 certification applications, and decrease Water Boards staffs' time spent on ensuring that impacts to waters are addressed and appropriately mitigated and monitored. Improved alignment of federal and state jurisdictional waters will also likely decrease permit processing time to the benefit of applicants.

In addition to these general comments, please find our specific comments on the language of the Proposed Rule in Attachment B to this letter. We appreciate the Agencies' outreach to state agencies in discussing this rulemaking effort and encourage the Agencies to continue to consult with the states as the Agencies consider the public comments and the rulemaking moves forward. Once the rulemaking is final, we encourage continued early outreach and coordination, particularly when making jurisdictional determinations pursuant to the newly-adopted "Waters of the United States" rule.

Thank you for considering these comments. If you have any questions regarding this submittal, please do not hesitate to call Bill Orme, Chief of the State Water Resources Control Board's Water Quality Certification Unit, at (916) 341–5464. You may also email him at: Bill.Orme@waterboards.ca.gov.

Sincerely,

THOMAS HOWARD,
Executive Director.

Attachment A

STREAMS AND WATERBODIES IN CALIFORNIA
THE NATIONAL HYDROGRAPHY DATASET

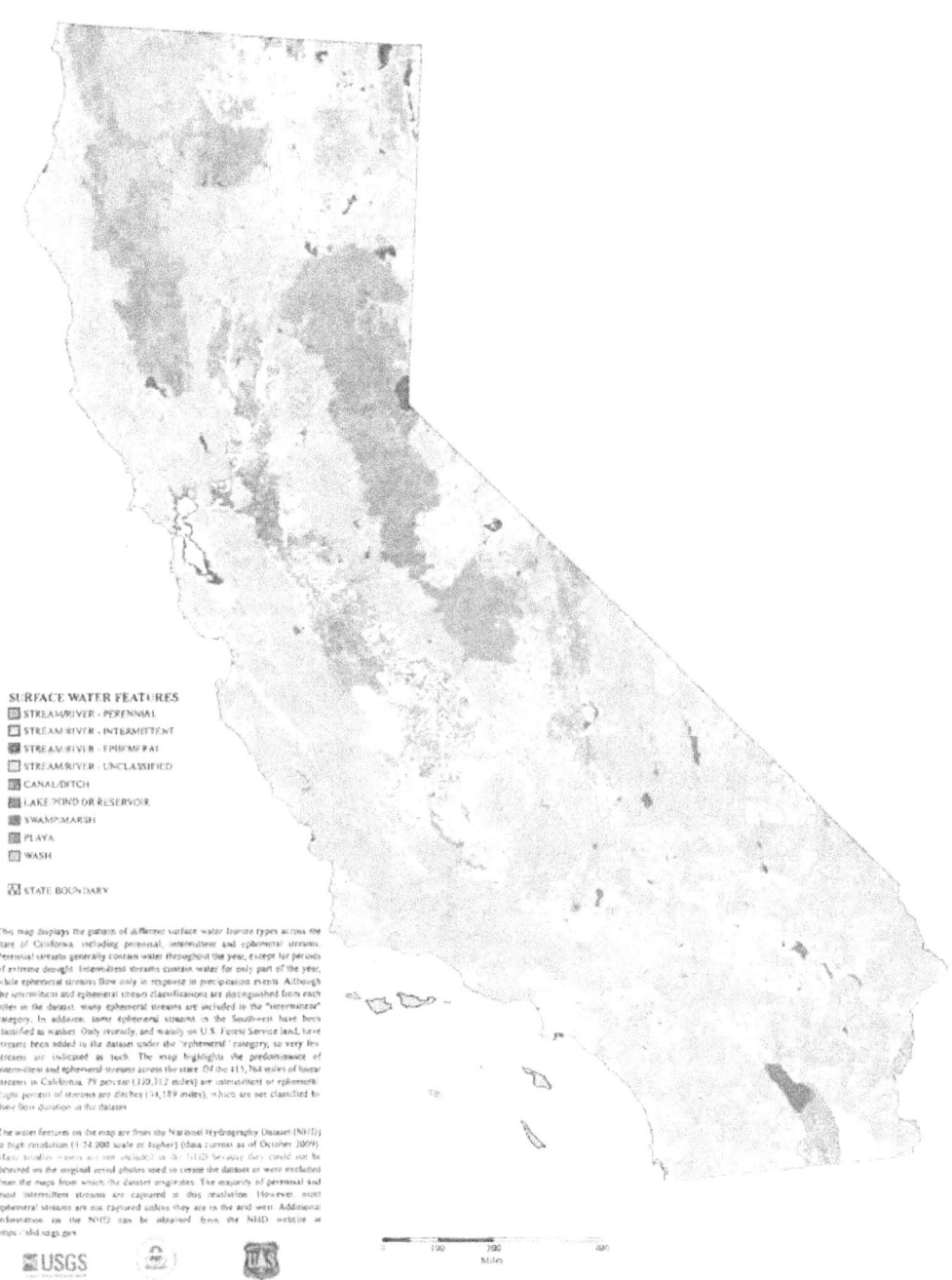

SURFACE WATER FEATURES
- STREAM/RIVER - PERENNIAL
- STREAM/RIVER - INTERMITTENT
- STREAM/RIVER - EPHEMERAL
- STREAM/RIVER - UNCLASSIFIED
- CANAL/DITCH
- LAKE/POND OR RESERVOIR
- SWAMP/MARSH
- PLAYA
- WASH

STATE BOUNDARY

This map displays the pattern of different surface water feature types across the state of California, including perennial, intermittent and ephemeral streams. Perennial streams generally contain water throughout the year, except for periods of extreme drought. Intermittent streams contain water for only part of the year, while ephemeral streams flow only in response to precipitation events. Although the intermittent and ephemeral stream classifications are distinguished from each other in the dataset, many ephemeral streams are included in the "intermittent" category. In addition, some ephemeral streams in the South-west have been classified as washes. Only recently, and mainly on U.S. Forest Service land, have streams been added to the dataset under the "ephemeral" category, so very few streams are collected as such. The map highlights the predominance of intermittent and ephemeral streams across the state. Of the 415,764 miles of linear streams in California, 79 percent (329,312 miles) are intermittent or ephemeral. Eight percent of streams are ditches (34,189 miles), which are not classified by their flow duration in this dataset.

The water features on the map are from the National Hydrography Dataset (NHD) at high resolution (1:24,000 scale or higher) (data current as of October 2009). Many smaller waters are not included in the NHD because they could not be detected on the original aerial photos used to create the dataset or were excluded from the maps from which the dataset originates. The majority of perennial and most intermittent streams are captured at this resolution. However, most ephemeral streams are not captured unless they are in the arid west. Additional information on the NHD can be obtained from the NHD website at https://nhd.usgs.gov

USGS

Attachment B

The following specific comments are provided by the California State Water Resources Control Board and the nine California regional water quality control boards (collectively, the "Water Boards") staff regarding the proposed "Definition of 'Waters of the United States' Under the Clean Water Act" (Proposed Rule) for 40 CFR 230.3. Specific recommended changes to the proposed regulations are shown in ~~strikeout~~/underline format. Additional comments are presented as endnotes.

Proposed "Definition of 'Waters of the United States' Under the Clean Water Act"
40 CFR 230.3

(s) For purposes of all sections of the Clean Water Act, 33 U.S.C. 1251 *et seq.* and its implementing regulations, subject to the exclusions in paragraph (t) of this section, the term "waters of the United States" means:

(1) All waters which are currently used, were used in the past, or may be susceptible to use in interstate or foreign commerce, including all waters which are subject to the ebb and flow of the tide;

(2) All interstate waters, including interstate wetlands;

(3) The territorial seas;

(4) All impoundments of waters identified in paragraphs (s)(1) through (3) and (5) of this section;

(5) All tributaries of waters identified in paragraphs (s)(1) through (4) of this section;

(6) All waters, including wetlands, adjacent to a water identified in paragraphs (s)(1) through (5) of this section; and

(7) On a case-specific basis, other waters, including wetlands, provided that those waters alone, or in combination with other similarly situated waters, including wetlands, located in the same region, have a significant nexus to a water identified in paragraphs (s)(1) through (3) of this section.

(t) The following are not "waters of the United States" notwithstanding whether they meet the terms of paragraphs (s)(1) through (7) of this section—

(1) Waste treatment systems, including treatment ponds, ~~or~~ lagoons, and storm water detention basins,[1] designed and used[2] to meet the requirements of the Clean Water Act and not constructed in a waters of the United States.[3]

(2) Prior converted cropland. Notwithstanding the determination of an area's status as prior converted cropland by any other Federal agency, for the purposes of the Clean Water Act the final authority regarding Clean Water Act jurisdiction remains with EPA.

(3) Ditches that are excavated wholly in uplands, drain only uplands, and have less than ~~perennial~~ intermittent[4] flow.

(4) Ditches that do not contribute flow, either directly or through another water, to a water identified in paragraphs (s)(1) through (4) of this section.

(5) The following features:

(i) Artificially irrigated areas that would revert to upland should application of irrigation water to that area cease;

(ii) Artificial lakes or ponds created by excavating and/or diking dry land and used exclusively for such purposes as stock watering, irrigation, settling basins, or rice growing;

(iii) Artificial reflecting pools or swimming pools created by excavating and/or diking dry land;

(iv) Small ornamental waters created by excavating and/or diking dry land for primarily aesthetic reasons;

(v) Water-filled depressions created incidental to construction activity that are not part of an interconnected network of waters of the United States;[5]

(vi) Groundwater, including groundwater drained through subsurface drainage systems; and

(vii) Gullies and rills and non-wetland swales.[6]

(u) Definitions—

(1) *Adjacent.* The term *adjacent* means bordering, contiguous or neighboring. Waters, including wetlands, separated from other waters of the United States by man-made dikes or barriers, natural river berms, beach dunes and the like are "adjacent waters."

(2) *Neighboring.* The term *neighboring,* for purposes of the term "adjacent" in this section, includes waters located within the riparian area or floodplain of a water identified in paragraphs (s)(1) through (5) of this section, or waters with a shallow subsurface hydrologic connection[7] or confined surface hydrologic connection to such a jurisdictional water.

(3) *Riparian area.* The term *riparian area* means an area bordering a water where surface or subsurface hydrology directly influence the ecological processes and plant and animal community structure in that area. Riparian areas are transitional areas between aquatic and terrestrial ecosystems that influence the exchange of energy and materials between those ecosystems.[8]

(4) *Floodplain.* The term *floodplain* means an area bordering inland or coastal waters that was formed by sediment deposition from such water under present climatic conditions and is inundated during periods of moderate to high water flows.

(5) *Tributary.* The term *tributary* means a water physically characterized by the presence of a bed and banks and ordinary high water mark, as defined at 33 CFR 328.3(e), which contributes flow, either directly or through another water, to a water identified in paragraphs (s)(1) through (4) of this section. In addition, wetlands[9] lakes, and ponds are tributaries (even if they lack a bed and banks or ordinary high water mark) if they contribute flow, either directly or through another water to a water identified in paragraphs (s)(1) through (3) of this section. A water that otherwise qualifies as a tributary under this definition does not lose its status as a tributary if, for any length, there are one or more man-made breaks (such as bridges, culverts, pipes, or dams), or one or more natural breaks (such as wetlands at the head of or along the run of a stream, natural discontinuous channels in dryland stream systems,[10] debris piles, boulder fields, or a stream that flows underground) so long as a bed and banks and an ordinary high water mark can be identified upstream of the break. A tributary, including wetlands, can be a natural, man-altered, or man-made water and includes waters such as rivers, streams, lakes, ponds, impoundments, canals, and ditches not excluded in paragraph (t)(3) or (4) of this section.

(6) *Wetlands.* The term *wetlands* means those areas that are inundated or saturated by surface or groundwater at a frequency and duration sufficient to support, and that under normal circumstances do support, a prevalence of vegetation typically adapted for life in

saturated soil conditions. Wetlands generally include swamps, marshes, bogs and similar areas.

(7) *Significant nexus.* The term *significant nexus* means that a water, including wetlands, either alone or in combination with other similarly situated waters in the region (i.e., the watershed that drains to the nearest water identified in paragraphs (s)(1) through (3) of this section), significantly affects the chemical, physical, or biological integrity of a water identified in paragraphs (s)(1) through (3) of this section. For an effect to be significant, it must be more than speculative or insubstantial. Other waters, including wetlands, are similarly situated when they perform similar functions and are located sufficiently close together or sufficiently close to a "water of the United States" so that they can be evaluated as a single landscape unit with regard to their effect on the chemical, physical, or biological integrity of a water identified in paragraphs (s)(1) through (3) of this section.[11]

---

[1] Stormwater detention basins and other constructed water-dependent stormwater treatment systems should also qualify for this exclusion.

[2] If a waste treatment system is abandoned or otherwise ceases to serve the treatment function it was designed for, it should not continue to qualify for the exclusion.

[3] Generally, waste treatment systems that are constructed within a water of the United States should not qualify for this exclusion. There may be some existing waste treatment systems that were constructed within a water of the United States that the Agencies affirmatively determined ceased to be a water of the United States; those determinations should remain in effect.

[4] The distinction between ditches excluded under proposed (t)(3) and ditches that meet the proposed definition of "tributary" is not clear, because "tributary" includes man-made ditches. If the ditch is not connected to a water of the United States and is not abandoned, then the flow regime may not be relevant. For ditches that are connected to waters of the United States, if the intent of the proposed (t)(3) exclusion is to be consistent with the significant nexus test, then an intermittent flow regime would be more appropriate than a permanent flow regime, particularly for arid and semi-arid areas. Alternatively, the simplest approach may be to treat all ditches that are excavated wholly in uplands and drain only uplands as potential point sources, rather than waters of the United States, without regard to flow regime. This approach could be limited to ditches that are not abandoned, and would include the upland portions of municipal separate storm sewer systems.

[5] There are cases where after a number of years of inactivity, water filled depressions created incidental to construction activity become habitat for plants and animals and support other designated uses. These water-filled depressions may be considered to be waters of the United States if they are interconnected with other waters of the United States.

[6] Non-wetland swales that contribute flow to waters of the United States may be considered waters of the United States. See endnote 9.

[7] We support the proposed definition of "neighboring." However, guidance should be provided on how to determine whether there is a "shallow subsurface hydrologic connection" for the purpose of this exclusion

[8] We support the definition of "riparian," because it is consistent with scientific evidence that riparian areas are areas through which surface and subsurface hydrology interconnect aquatic

areas and connect them with their adjacent uplands (Brinson et al., 2002). They are distinguished by gradients in biophysical conditions, ecological processes, and biota. They can include wetlands, aquatic support areas, and portions of uplands that significantly influence the conditions or processes of aquatic areas.

[9] We support the proposed language including wetlands as tributary. However, the Agencies should consider whether interconnecting non-wetland swales that provide critical hydrologic connectivity to wetland complexes should be excluded. In California, this is commonly found in vernal pool complexes. Although vernal pools may be considered jurisdictional, swales that provide chemical, physical, and biological connectivity would be excluded. For clarity, we suggest that the Agencies consider whether to add "interconnecting swales" to clarify that interconnecting swales in wetland complexes should be considered jurisdictional because they directly contribute flows and function as part of the tributary system to waters of the United States.

We agree that gullies and rills, and non-wetland swales in upland areas that are purely erosional features and do not contribute flow, either directly or through another water, to waters of the United States correctly should not be considered jurisdictional by rule. However, as suggested by the Scientific Advisory Board, the Agencies should consider whether non-wetland swales in arid and semi-arid environments and low gradient landscapes should be included as tributaries if they contribute flow to waters of the United States (particularly headwaters in zero order basins), regardless of the presence of an ordinary high water mark. There are many ephemeral and intermittent tributaries in the arid West, such as those ephemeral channels that are tributary to the Mojave River and Amargosa River in California. As shown on the National Hydrography Dataset (NHD) high resolution map (Attachment A), the majority of streams in California (79 percent) are intermittent or ephemeral (INDUS Corporation, 2013).

Headwaters undergo geomorphic processes, such as erosion and incision, which may take the initial form of non-wetland swales. Therefore, these headwater features can significantly affect the chemical, physical, and biological integrity of waters of the United States. The importance of headwater stream systems is noted throughout the preamble to the Proposed Rule on page 22201: "The great majority of tributaries are headwater streams, and whether they are perennial, intermittent, or ephemeral, they play an important role in the transport of water, sediments, organic matter, nutrients, and organisms to downstream environments. Tributaries serve to store water, thereby reducing flooding, provide biogeochemical functions that help maintain water quality, trap and transport sediments, transport, store and modify pollutants, provide habitat for plants and animals, and sustain the biological productivity of downstream rivers, lakes and estuaries." Additionally, the preamble to the Proposed Rule clearly recognizes on page 22206 the benefits of headwater and ephemeral streams: "[t]ributaries that are small, flow infrequently, or are a substantial distance from the nearest (a)(1) through (a)(3) water (e.g., headwater perennial, intermittent, and ephemeral tributaries) are essential components of the tributary network and have important effects on the chemical, physical, and biological integrity of (a)(1) through (a)(3) waters, contributing many of the same functions downstream as larger streams. When their functional contributions to the chemical, physical, and biological conditions of downstream waters are considered at a watershed scale, the scientific evidence supports a legal determination that they meet the "significant nexus" standard articulated by Justice Kennedy in *Rapanos*."

[10] We note that there are ephemeral and intermittent streams in arid and semi-arid regions that are commonly referred to as "drylands" (Levick et al., 2008; CDFG, 2010). Natural

discontinuous channels in dryland stream ephemeral channels are characterized by alternating erosional and depositional reaches that may vary in length (USACE, 2008). These channels are constantly in flux and are characterized by temporal and spatial changes in channel morphology for any given location. These systems are subject to prolonged wet and dry cycles and typically have many years of discontinuous flows. Since jurisdiction should be based on physical structure rather than the vagaries of climate, these features when contributing flow either directly or through another water to a water of the United States, should be considered jurisdictional.

[11] We support the proposed "significant nexus" definition, including specifically, "a water, including wetlands, either alone or in combination with other similarly situated waters in the region (i.e., the watershed that drains to the nearest water identified in paragraphs (s)(1) through (3) of this section), significantly affects the chemical, physical, or biological integrity of a water identified in paragraphs (s)(1) through (3) of this section." Making the determination of "similarly situated" waters should be done at the watershed level (for these purposes, the term watershed should mean all areas resulting from the first subdivision of a subbasin). Certainty that waters are "similarly situated" and thus similarly affecting the chemical, physical, or biological integrity of jurisdictional waters increases when the area of analysis is confined to a watershed where, by definition, all waters flow to a common point. Although waters within an ecoregion could similarly affect chemical, physical, or biological integrity of a jurisdictional water, the large scale of ecoregions would greatly complicate the analysis and provide more opportunities for challenges to the jurisdictional determinations.

In addition, we recommend that the Agencies make it clear that the existence of a significant nexus may be reassessed in cases where new permanent changes in hydrology occur, through natural or man caused events (e.g., climate change), altering hydrologic flows. In such cases, a water previously determined not to be jurisdictional under the rule, may be found to be jurisdictional in its new altered condition.

Literature Cited

Brinson, M. M. et al. (2002). *Riparian Areas: Functions and Strategies for Management.* Washington, D.C: National Academy Press.

California Department of Fish and Game (CDFG). (2010). *A review of Stream Processes and Forms in Dryland Watersheds.* Prepared by K. Vyverberg, Senior Engineering Geologist, Conservation Engineering. December 2010.

INDUS Corporation. (2013). *Streams and Waterbodies in California The NHD Dataset:*

U.S. Army Corps of Engineers (USACE). (2008). *A Field Guide to the Identification of the Ordinary High Water Mark (OHWM) in the Arid West Region of the Western United States.* R. W. Lichvar, and S. M. McColley. ERDC/CRREL TR-08-12. August 2008.

Levick, L. J. et al. (2008). *The Ecological and Hydrological Significance of Ephemeral and Intermittent Streams in the Arid and Semi-arid American Southwest.* U.S. Environmental Protection Agency and U.S. Department of Agriculture/ARS Southwest Watershed Research Center.

————

[LIST OF DOCUMENTS SUBMITTED FOR THE RECORD RETAINED IN THE COMMITTEE'S OFFICIAL FILES]

— National Wildlife Federation—Prepared Statement
— National Association of Realtors®—Prepared Statement